Schumann

A Listener's Guide

Victor Lederer

AMADEUS
PRESS
An Imprint of Hal Leonard LLC

Published in 2017 by Amadeus Press
An Imprint of Hal Leonard LLC
7777 West Bluemound Road
Milwaukee, WI 53213

Trade Book Division Editorial Offices
33 Plymouth St., Montclair, NJ 07042

Printed in the United States of America

Book design by Snow Creative

Library of Congress Cataloging-in-Publication Data

Names: Lederer, Victor, author.
Title: Schumann : a listener's guide / Victor Lederer.
Description: Milwaukee, WI : Amadeus Press, 2017. | Series: Unlocking the masters series ; no. 29 | Includes bibliographical references.
Identifiers: LCCN 2016046213 | ISBN 9781574674880
Subjects: LCSH: Schumann, Robert, 1810–1856—Criticism and interpretation. | Music—19th century—History and criticism.
Classification: LCC ML410.S4 L3954 2017 | DDC 780.92—dc23
LC record available at https://lccn.loc.gov/2016046213

www.amadeuspress.com

Schumann

Unlocking the Masters Series, No. 29

Series Editor: Robert Levine

For Elaine, again

Contents

Acknowledgments

Thanks to my children, Karen, Paul, and Kate, as well as to Richard Thypin and Nancy Bermeo. Lambert Orkis's thoughts about the piano trios were insightful and are much appreciated. Thanks to my good-humored editor and friend, Bob Levine. Special thanks as always to my teacher and friend Bernie Rose, whose love of Schumann's music revived my own enthusiasm, which occasionally flagged.

Schumann

1 Understanding Schumann

Although much of Robert Schumann's work is familiar, especially to audiences of music for the piano, his output is much wider than the piano concerto and the dozen or so solo keyboard hits. To the small audience for art song, he's as important as any composer, including Franz Schubert, whom he may even surpass in influence and quality, as Schumann wrote fewer songs and was more selective about the texts he set. But while most music lovers may know that he's supreme in that field, it's simply not one with a wide following. His chamber music, with two or three exceptions, does not stand with what most consider as crucial in that noble category. Even with flaws that are undeniable, his four symphonies are all well liked. His dramatic works, chiefly the opera *Genoveva* and the Incidental Music to Byron's *Manfred*, are rarely performed and little known. There seems to be at least three Schumanns: the wild, sometimes undisciplined genius of the early piano works; the lyrical but impassioned master of lied (song) and finally the ever more conservative—sometimes bland and stodgy—postclassicist.

In addition to Schumann's obvious qualities, which include a rare originality, inspired melodic invention, warmth of feeling, and a daring strangeness, most musicians and music lovers have long been aware of several undeniable flaws. These stem from his difficulties with form and management of his material. With so many of the great piano works consisting of tiny, sketchlike pieces strung together, it's tempting to call him a miniaturist out of his depth in larger forms. But that would be wrong: in his best works for piano and in the great song cycles, the paradoxical Schumann assembles his material with uncanny skill for contrast between the character pieces or songs that make them up, providing a sense of powerful, inevitable flow from beginning to end.

Several more or less contemporaneous early piano works highlight this paradox. The eight movements of *Kreisleriana* are neither short nor long and ordered flawlessly, with each of its dramatic, demonic, and lyrical sections served in its turn and correct place, all essential elements of a grandly overarching structure (like several others, the title is a literary reference I'll explain in chapter 3). There's not another musical work like it. Also in eight movements, the *Fantasiestücke*—"Fantasy Pieces"—are far less integrally connected and perhaps less even in quality, too. Many consider the multipart *Humoreske* a failure of organization, in spite of the undeniable beauty of some of its material. Yet the early piano suites built of short sections that are linked but contrasting (*Papillons, Davidsbündlertänze, Carnaval, Kinderszenen*) are formidable structural achievements as well as lyrical utterances, and justly beloved for their pacing and flow as much as for the charm, originality, and power of their material. If you haven't heard the composer's sixteen-song cycle *Dichterliebe*, you may well be in for a life-changing discovery: like Schubert's great cycles, *Die schöne Müllerin* and *Winterreise*, it seems impossible to improve on, in no small part thanks to its flawless organization.

The fact is that Schumann's oeuvre is uneven, even wildly so. Revisionist attempts of the last few decades to rehabilitate neglected masterpieces from the latter part of his career have turned up few. For many musicians and listeners, the view that Schumann was an early bloomer whose best and most exciting creations came early still seems to hold. Yet even in these old favorites there's sometimes a sense that Schumann gets stuck on an idea, or obsessively spins notes. This characteristic can be heard even in works of unquestionable greatness, such as the *Études symphoniques*. Sometimes, as in the Piano Sonata No. 1, and the final section of the *Études*, he repeats a single rhythmic figure obsessively, the result for some listeners a brutal, unvaried pummeling. At a textural level the *Études* also reveal a mannerism Schumann shares with many composers, phrasing that's foursquare and lacking in variety.

Looked at another way, a key element in the popularity of the great suites of short character pieces (particularly the *Davidsbündlertänze* and *Carnaval*) are the joint perfection of material and pacing, and of rhythmic variety with many displaying a sense of propulsive acceleration that's singular to this composer. It's possible of course that the tastes of musicians and audiences will widen to accommodate other works of Schumann's into the canon that are great, or close to it. It has happened before: in *Music for the Piano*, a respected, entertaining, and generally reliable 1954 guide to the piano literature by two piano teachers at the Juilliard School, the shocking suggestion to amputate much of the *Davidsbündlertänze*[1] is made. If authors James Friskin and Irwin Freundlich couldn't hear the near perfection of this eighteen-movement suite, with its heart-stopping reprise toward the end of ideas from earlier in the piece, then anything is possible.

Schumann belonged to a remarkable generation of composers, including Mendelssohn, Chopin, Liszt, Berlioz, Wagner, and Verdi, who cover an immense formal and stylistic range; their contributions to the repertory are correspondingly enormous. It's interesting, for instance, to compare Schumann with Frédéric Chopin, the great Polish composer who focused only on the piano, and whose works, along with Schumann's, form the heart of the nineteenth-century keyboard repertory. While both made contributions that are crucial, the differences between the two are striking. As Charles Rosen, a brilliant musicologist and pianist who died in 2012, observed:

> Although [Schumann] was perhaps the most original composer of the 1830s and 1840s, he was less capable than Chopin. That is, his music is less perfect than Chopin's, and more difficult to perform. There are not many pieces of Chopin which don't work in concert . . . But there are pieces of Schumann—very great works like the *Humoreske*, the F-sharp Minor Sonata and the F Minor Sonata—which don't really come off well in concert but are very great and original in context and form.[2]

Chopin was a ruthless editor of his own work, always paring, clearing textures and tightening, always making even the most beautiful of his ideas carry their weight structurally, and scrupulously publishing only his best work. Chopin's style grew more complex, but there's an obvious development from what came before, with early, middle, and late Chopin all in his characteristic and inimitable manner. Schumann's love of some of his ideas is obvious from how he lingers over them, as is his lack of severity in deciding what to publish. While we may find late works by Schumann attractive, the sense of a progressing style as with Chopin is lacking. Artists act as their lives and talents demand, but it's hard not to sense the loss of Schumann's early originality and fire. Rosen raises another crucial point regarding Schumann's mental state and late revisions he made to early works. The composer died in a mental hospital in 1856, having attempted suicide two years earlier. The chapter that follows will relate the history of his deterioration and death, but Schumann himself seems to have known something was wrong, fearing insanity for years before that catastrophic breakdown. In an attempt to fend off his madness, whether real or perceived (is there a difference?), the composer revised his early music, hoping to tame what was wild and regularize the irregular, both of which are major elements in their greatness:

> I think he went through his old pieces and removed anything that could be interpreted as evidence of insanity—anything very original, eccentric, or peculiar. He took out at least two of the greatest details of the *Kreisleriana*. And in the case of the *Davidsbündlertänze*, Schumann altered some of the greatest things in the piece. New editions of Schumann that are coming out are all based on the last text, and they should really be based on the first one.[3]

Of course, it's impossible to find a moment in his work when Schumann's insanity, or his fear of it, is manifest in the music, but the tendency away from the wild and rhapsodic toward regular, larger scale, more conventional forms and tamer thematic material is obvious, and even if you're new to the music, you'll know the difference when you hear it. Front-end loaded with masterpieces of inimitable personality, the early years of Schumann's career are remarkable for their daring and appeal, as a look at a chronological list of his works readily reveals. I was even tempted to divide the keyboard works (a large subgroup within Schumann's oeuvre) into chapters for lesser and greater, so clear is the difference; but ultimately it seemed better to be objective and treat them chronologically.

One of the most powerful characteristics of Schumann's early music is its bipolar quality. The composer's early character pieces for piano are made of short sections, with the fiery and energetic ones identified as "Florestan," symbolizing one side of his personality, and the dreamy, introspective sections with which they alternate identified with the name "Eusebius." In an early edition Schumann marked each number in the *Davidsbündlertänze*—"Dances of the Band of David"—with an "F" or "E" to show which side of his personality was engaged. These are among the indications he removed later, even though the differences between the two are key to the work's effect and quite evident once you've heard it. Several sections also contained short commentaries, rather like stage directions, which were also removed. The equally great *Carnaval* also alternates lively and introspective pieces, with portraits of musicians and others the composer knew as a key to the undying popularity of that astonishing work. The point is that Schumann came by his bipolarity naturally, applying it with wit and genius in these and other pieces, and that he very possibly was clinically bipolar in the modern sense. The composer moves convincingly and with consummate skill between these personae, and others, too.

Several of the great early piano works can be viewed as radical expansions of the dance suites of Schubert, with the earliest, *Papillons*, standing closest to the Schubertian model. But even that work contains ironies not to be found in Schubert's straightforward dance sets; *Carnaval* and the *Davidsbündlertänze* make enormous leaps in originality and strangeness, although echoes of Schubert can be heard even in these works.

The title *Davidsbündlertänze* refers to an imaginary band of warriors fighting the trite and banal in European music of the day; the literary side of Schumann's mental life and process was perhaps larger and more telling than with any important composer. Almost everything he composed in his early years has a literary inspiration of some kind, and Schumann's own critical writings form an extremely important aspect of his life and work. His father was a successful publisher and book merchant, providing early nurturing for his son's bookish ways. Literary by inclination, Schumann was a talented writer and a critic as well as a composer, well known for his unselfish praise of the music of

Chopin and Brahms, with the latter eventually becoming a close friend. It was in his role as a reviewer that Schumann famously and quite correctly wrote of Chopin, "Hats off, gentlemen, a genius!"[4] As a founder of the musical journal *Neue Zeitschrift für Musik*—"New Magazine for Music"—in 1833, Schumann took up the cause of progressive composers. For the sake of Brahms, he resumed critical writing in 1853, ten years after his last review. Although not as quotably pithy as his praise of Chopin, Schumann's words on Brahms were equally fervent. But by then Schumann's own music had changed, as he praised Brahms, his musical heir and who even when young was a confirmed formalist. But the original purpose of the *Neue Zeitschrift* was to stand in opposition to conservative and parochial music journals, bravely covering compositions from across Europe and even from the Western Hemisphere.[5]

There's some sense, then, behind Schumann's own early originality in form, as he saw the old forms—sonata, variation, and concerto—in decline. His return to classical structures seems like a weakness, but was perhaps inevitable given the boldness and originality of the early works: how many *Carnaval*s or *Kreisleriana*s can one composer turn out? Again, comparison with Chopin may be helpful. That master worked in the same forms (waltz, nocturne, mazurka, scherzo, ballade, and others) repeatedly over the course of his career. But these more neutral vessels allowed Chopin to develop his stylistic trademarks—memorable in melodic profile and bold in harmony and rhythm—richly within them. Schumann's early daring was in a way an impossible foundation for a lifetime career as a composer.

And in fact, three sprawling but passionate piano sonatas stand alongside the *Carnaval* and other suites among the composer's early works. He obviously wanted from the start to revive the form and to infuse it with a new energy. As we'll see, Schumann's ambitions for these outran his organizational abilities, but even so all three contain much fine material. One, the very difficult F Minor, Op. 14, has by now entered the repertory as an occasional item, if not exactly a staple.

So potent is the influence of music on our nervous systems that we imagine more in the way of wild inspiration than composers actually experience, difficult as their creative work may be. Reports by friends and students of Beethoven's struggles with recalcitrant material may have reinforced this idea. But there's far more method to musical composition than many realize, closer to Ravel's remark to the effect that first he tried one note, then another. The key variables in it are melody, rhythm, harmony, and the means of delivery, whether voice, piano, instrumental ensemble, alone or in countless combinations. Schumann was not alone in beginning works in improvisation at the keyboard: Haydn worked the same way. But ultimately every composer has to select the notes he or she wants and write them down. Schumann's techniques changed as he aged, and varied based on the form in which he worked. As we'll see, the more traditional forms of the chamber and symphonic works required traditional ways of working the ideas out. Interestingly, he wrote songs in a different manner, devising the melody away from the piano, then adding the keyboard accompaniment.[6]

Schumann played the piano a great deal, impressing many who heard him with his skill—or perhaps something beyond it—at improvisation. Many of his early works for piano—the *Fantasie, Kreisleriana*, and the *Arabeske*, for example—display moments of freedom that can only have begun as improvisations. Even more unusual is the long, free postlude for piano to the last song in the *Dichterliebe* cycle, which sounds like a natural musical commentary on the sung texts that preceded, a song without words at the highest expressive pitch. This is one of Schumann's boldest inspirations, seeming to arrive out of the blue, and staying fresh even once you know it's coming. Paradoxically, there's another aspect of that freedom to be heard in other works, which also sound improvised but feel as though subjected to insufficient tightening and editing. Moments of freedom like these ultimately disappeared as Schumann became more reliant on forms.

Yet even those who wish Schumann had maintained the daring of his early years will likely find themselves seduced by the ardor and warmth of such works as the Piano Quartet, the Piano Quintet, and the Piano Trio No. 1. The symphonies may be imperfect, but they contain much fine material. As you listen to and learn about the composer, you can expect at least a few unfamiliar gems to emerge. Going through Schumann's oeuvre can be a bumpy ride, but at his best he sounds thrillingly like no one else.

2 Schumann's Life

There's a remarkable amount of speculation on a life as well documented as Schumann's. No two biographies seem to take the same point of view, with some making wild leaps of assumption. What sparks many hypotheses are the insanity that unquestionably struck the composer two years before his death, when he attempted suicide, its causes and the possibility of earlier manifestations. The composer himself expressed a fear of madness with regularity and ever greater intensity as the years passed. His diaries as well as the memories of his wife, Clara, also have given rise to a great deal of embroidery and speculation. A sensible if unverified explanation to his sharp decline at age forty-four and death two years later is syphilis, an illness that was misunderstood and untreatable by nineteenth-century medicine, which he seems to have contracted from a girlfriend when he was twenty.

Schumann was born on June 8, 1810, into a bourgeois family in the small city of Zwickau, in the east-central German province of Saxony—Sachsen in German. He was the last of six children born to August and Johanne Schumann, affluent members of the middle class. August was an enterprising writer, editor, translator, and seller of books and newspapers, and surely it was from him that Robert developed his own love of reading and formidable skill as a writer. Schumann's early years are remarkable only for their ordinariness, as he was apparently doted on by his parents and siblings as the baby of the clan. Like many musicians—but also like many children—he was attracted by musical instruments and the sounds they made; as did many of his era and class, he took piano lessons with a local teacher of modest abilities. As a relatively small and isolated town, Zwickau was not a musical center like nearby Leipzig or Dresden, and Schumann would eventually realize how unimpressive his teacher Johann Kuntsch's skills at the keyboard were.

Schumann's own playing improved, however, as did a gift at improvising that impressed listeners for most of the rest of his life. This was a time when the ability to improvise was a major element in a musician's skill set, even though he wasn't yet set on the track to be a pianist or a composer. But even as a boy, Schumann wrote little dances for his sisters. His playing was so good that his father bought a grand piano for him as a gift, a touching gesture that shows the warmth in the family, the values it held, and its affluence, too. At twelve he composed a choral setting to Psalm 150, while telling his parents that the poorly trained Kuntsch's lessons were no longer helpful.[1] Schumann's own character seems already to have been strong willed and self-directed, doing what he wanted with passion while dodging responsibilities he disliked. Even as an adolescent, Schumann's future as a musician was still unclear, an unusual circumstance for a major composer. He loved music, but his bookishness also drew him to fiction and poetry. Like many artistically inclined adolescents he wrote flowery verse in the prevailing style of the era, and he began to keep journals and diaries, as well. The difficult German novelist Jean Paul (the pen name for Johann Paul Friedrich Richter), and later E. T. A. Hoffmann, whose demonic tales and novels paralleled the work of Edgar Allan Poe, were important influences on the young Schumann. As with Poe, Hoffmann's influence would loom large across Western culture for decades, well into the twentieth century. As we'll see in the next chapter, the title of *Kreisleriana*, one of the composer's greatest keyboard works, is a reference and tribute to Hoffmann.

August Schumann died in 1826, and Robert's mother sent him to study law at the University of Heidelberg two years later. Although unsure whether his future lay as a literary man or a musician, Robert seems to have felt from the start that the law was not for him. He liked student life well, however, drinking too much (according to his own diaries), taking up cigars, and overspending. Although he didn't like the law, he attended at least some lectures, making friends with other students and members of the faculty.

While at Heidelberg, Schumann decided that his well-appreciated piano playing was the direction for him after all. He approached Leipzig piano teacher Friedrich Wieck, a sophisticated musician with a taste for the avant-garde of the day (Chopin, for example) and the father of Clara Wieck, a child prodigy pianist, for help in polishing his technique and bringing his artistry up to a higher level. Once Wieck had accepted him as a pupil, Schumann had great difficulty in persuading his mother that music was the path for him, for exactly the same reasons middle-class parents today fear musical careers for their children. Eventually she gave in, as Wieck promised to let her know after six months whether Robert had a chance at success.

In some ways the years Schumann spent in Leipzig as a student and associate of Wieck's were the pivotal ones of his life. His friendship and alliance with Wieck would end in mutual hatred as he and Clara, who was nine years younger, fell in love. They would marry only after enormous battles with Friedrich. Finally, it seems credible that Schumann contracted syphilis from his girlfriend of the time, referred to in his diaries alternatively as "Christel" and "Charitas."[2] Nothing more is known about her, but their proximity makes it likely that she was likely a domestic of some sort in the Wieck household.[3] The disease, which is contagious only for a period after contraction, was never passed to Clara or any of the seven children she and Robert had. But apparently it did return catastrophically twenty-three years later to destroy Schumann.

For all Wieck's strengths as teacher there were two factors neither Schumann nor any pupil could overcome: Wieck's primary focus on Clara's playing and career, and his fierce and unpredictable temper. Nevertheless, pupil and teacher started out liking each other and even working together as contributors to the *Neue Zeitschrift für Musik*—"New Magazine for Music"—the musical journal founded by Schumann and others and the vehicle for his early critical writings. As one of its founders, the young and idealistic musician devoted great energy to the enterprise; before long, however, he and his fellow writer-editors quarreled. As so often happens, one member takes on more responsibility, in this case Schumann, who before long felt the need to buy out his partners. A dedicated reader, Schumann was also a fine writer, and an astute, if not perfectly prescient critic; none are. Yet his vivid and imaginative prose still reads remarkably well. In general, Schumann saw the demise of older, classical forms, at least in their feeble incarnations of the time, and the concomitant birth of new ones. While he inevitably backed some now-forgotten names, in the 1830s, he placed himself firmly on the side of innovators, including Chopin and Berlioz. Florestan and Eusebius, the two imaginary sides of the composer's personality (both musical and literary), make their first appearances in his journals and diaries of the same years along with others who peopled his imagined band of fighters against the banal, which he dubbed the *Davidsbündler*—"Band of David"—a reference to the Old Testament hero and killer of Goliath.

It was also in 1831, while studying with Wieck, that Schumann used a mechanical device to strengthen the middle finger of his right hand. But the result was that the finger was crippled, thus ending his hopes of performing. It may also have been the outcome of overpracticing, causing what's now diagnosed as repetitive motion disorder. Schumann must have been quite a pianist, as the technical difficulty of much of the early piano works demonstrates. It's easy to say that a shift to composing was better for musical history, or that later he would have a great pianist as his wife to try out ideas he could no longer execute, but the loss of hope for a career was surely a source of pain and uncertainty to Schumann at the time. This was also a period during which excessive drinking was noted with depressing regularity in his journal.

These were also the months and years when Schumann's earliest work, all for piano, were published. He had conceived one, the Toccata, while a student in Heidelberg, but polished this murderously difficult showpiece and published it as his opus 7 in 1834. (*Opus* is Latin for "work"; many composers starting with Haydn and more systematically with Beethoven, published their compositions with opus numbers, abbreviated as *op.*) The first of Schumann's works to be published with an opus number is the impressive "ABEGG" Variations, in some ways a typical showpiece of the time, but with more depth and moments of the strangeness that characterizes the composer at his best. His opus 2 is even better, the sublime *Papillons*—"Butterflies"—a suite of twelve waltzes in the manner of Schubert, but with highly original echoes, disruptions, and ironies. As with the Toccata, Schumann assembled

Papillons from earlier sketches, polishing and refining them into something new and bold, with key changes that baffled its first hearers but seem to have impressed the twelve-year-old Clara Wieck. The juxtaposition of contrasting short sections in *Papillons* would pay off in a big way in *Carnaval* and *Davidsbündlertänze*, the great character suites for keyboard of 1834 and 1837, respectively.

Amid a couple of works of lower importance, Schumann began several big piano sonatas, of which he would ultimately complete and publish three. He also suffered in 1833 the first of several panic attacks that would be described in older biographies as nervous breakdowns. Schumann was certainly a hypochondriac, noting every ache in his diary, and bouts of illness seem frequent in any of his biographies. His family would become used to it, but of course it's possible that some of his ailments were the result of syphilis's taking its gradual toll as the disease worked its way through his nervous and vascular systems and joints. He had a somewhat unusual personality: sure of himself in his work but also extremely taciturn. After visiting Schumann, Richard Wagner called his host "impossible . . . you can't always talk alone."[4] For Wagner, who saw the world and everyone in it as mirrors of himself, the comment is revealing, as he liked to dominate conversations. For her part Clara sized Wagner up amusingly: "He never stops talking about himself, he's insufferably arrogant and is forever laughing in his whining tone."[5] Yet, Brahms, who came to know Schumann well, always spoke of him with admiration, writing for instance in a letter of 1873 that "I will always take this noble, pure artist as my model."[6]

Since Clara was only eleven when Schumann (then age twenty) came to study with her father, the relationship between the two seems, not surprisingly, to have been not unlike that of brother and sister. Schumann recognized Clara's gifts as a pianist, remarkable even then, and she admired his skill at improvisation as well as his own works when he performed them for Wieck. Schumann teased, played with, and felt protective toward Clara, who looked up to him. It wouldn't be a huge leap to assume that the young Clara had a crush on Schumann, but marriage to her was surely not his initial intention.

In 1834 and 1835 Schumann, an attractive and interesting man, developed a relationship with Ernestine von Fricken, also a student of

Wieck's, to whom he became engaged. He didn't love her, but she was certainly musical and supposedly a wealthy aristocrat. Schumann backed out as gracefully as he could when he discovered that Ernestine was in fact the illegitimate niece of her supposed father who had adopted her, and that she herself had no money. Clara watched all this with jealousy and then relief, as by this time she really did love Schumann, who in turn had begun to see her as the formidable, unconventionally beautiful woman she was becoming. At this point her career as a performer was starting, locally in and around Leipzig, but notice was favorable wherever she played. The contact between this protected young woman, who would become by all accounts one of the greatest pianists of her day, and the gifted young composer did finally turn amorous, although not sexually intimate. Friedrich Wieck erupted when he found out about their relationship, forbidding contact between the two, a sure way to provoke the strong-willed couple into staying in touch. Wieck sent Clara to Dresden for more advanced musical education, and of course to put distance between her and Schumann. But both Schumann and Clara had a stubborn streak with neither easily intimidated.

The story of how Robert and Clara overcame Friedrich Wieck's opposition is genuinely distressing. One must understand that Clara loved her father, who had made her into one of the most accomplished performers in Europe, and the only female pianist of the era to attain such heights. The break was most difficult on Clara, taking her far longer than Schumann, who was quite clear-eyed in this matter, to realize that Wieck would never willingly grant his consent. Surely the nasty and manipulative Wieck comes off worst, although many biographers point out that his opposition is understandable in light of the time, energy, skills as a teacher, and money he had devoted to Clara's career from when she was five years old.

After his initial blow-up, Wieck's shifted his strategy, telling the couple that he might approve, as long as Schumann could guarantee his income level, and puzzlingly, that if married, the couple could not live in Leipzig. Schumann did have an inheritance from his father, the interest of which he lived on; by 1837 there was some income from his published compositions, and there was a little money from sales of the *Neue Zeitchrift für Musik*, too. But even when he stretched the truth a little, Schumann was and probably would remain short of Wieck's financial bogey. Wieck was also willing to torment the more vulnerable Clara by undercutting her career, which by then was well on its way, by refusing to continue as her coach and manager. Sometimes irrational but too often calculating, Wieck tempted Clara with suggestions the sole intention of which were to separate her from Schumann, whose alcohol consumption, morals, and music he criticized, even though the two had often gone drinking together while Robert was his pupil, and he had in letters written of his admiration of Schumann as a pianist, composer, writer, and intellectual.[7]

This was also an era when expectations for morality were much higher for women than men, for daughters than for sons, and Wieck's rights over his eighteen-year-old daughter were surprisingly broad. He could legally deny her his approval, and Clara's only recourse was to appeal to the court for her independence. Finally, in July 1839 she unhappily took the step, as her father's behavior had finally gone beyond the pale for her—Schumann himself had long since figured out Wieck's game and explored with lawyers what could be done. As cunning a defendant as one might expect, Wieck used every trick including delaying to put off the court's decision, publishing vicious attacks on Schumann and even acting to undercut Clara's public image. There's no romanticizing the stresses the suit put on Robert and Clara's alliance, as disgust, pessimism and hopelessness overcame both at times. Finally, however, in January 1840, the court rendered a mixed verdict favoring Clara and Robert, later rejecting Wieck's appeal, and freeing Clara from her father's domination. Deadlines for appeals by Wieck ticked away over that summer, as the court announced its final verdict that granted Clara her independence on August 1, 1840. She and Robert were married on September 12.

In October 1838, partly in response to Wieck's odd insistence that they move from Leipzig, Schumann traveled to Vienna to find out whether that city might be one where he and Clara could settle. He stayed for six months, unhappy with the slow pace of the conservative imperial city's bureaucracies, notably the censors through whom all intellectual property had to be cleared, an environment far less free than Leipzig. He did, however, write some fine lighter piano works while there, including the *Arabeske*, Op. 18; the *Blumenstück*, Op. 19; as well as the underrated, Viennese-oriented *Faschingsschwank aus Wien*—"Carnival Scenes from Vienna"—Op. 26, and he pulled together the third of his piano sonatas, in G Minor, Op. 22. While in Vienna he also received from Franz Schubert's brother the then-unpublished Symphony No. 9, which he recognized as a masterwork and played a key role in restoring to the musical world, in itself a major achievement.

In spite of Schumann's struggles, or possibly thanks to them, the years spent battling Wieck were among his greatest, and for many listeners his very best. Anything started or completed in the phase from 1835 to 1840 Schumann tended to ascribe to his longing for Clara; the roll call includes such undisputed and varied masterworks for piano as the *Fantasie*, Op. 17, from 1836, and the *Davidsbündlertänze*, Op. 6, completed the following year. (The irregularities between opus numbers and dates of composition result from the fact that works were not necessarily published in the order in which they were written.) The composer wrestled with the majestic, if imperfect, set of variations *Études symphoniques*, Op. 13, from 1834 to 1837. The following year saw two keyboard suites of vastly different character, the tender but unsentimental *Kinderszenen*—"Scenes from Childhood"—Op. 15, and the demonic *Kreisleriana*, Op. 16. Eighteen forty is famous as Schumann's "year of song," because in less than twelve months, he composed more than 140, including his greatest. It was in 1840 that he wrote the cycles *Frauenliebe und -leben*—"A Woman's Life and Loves"—Op. 42; *Liederkreis*—literally, "Circle of Songs"—Op. 39; and best of all, the matchless *Dichterliebe*—"Poet's Love"—Op. 48, to poems of Heinrich Heine. Schumann's gift burned with a manic brightness, as for some weeks over that summer his average production of lieder (songs) was one per day.

No ordinary couple, the Schumanns shared their thoughts, feelings, and impressions in a joint diary, where more discretion than a private journal can be perceived. But they certainly seem to have been happy at the start of their marriage. Living in an apartment in a newer Leipzig neighborhood, the two musicians inspired and coached each other. Before long, and apparently on Clara's urging, and while still producing lieder, Schumann began two of his symphonies. Early in 1841 he started work on his Symphony No. 1, Op. 38, nicknamed "Spring" by the composer, a solid and still popular work. As was his way in this period, Schumann worked quickly and intensely. By this time Clara was pregnant with the first of the seven children she would bear. The composer Felix Mendelssohn had become their friend, and this gifted all-around musician helped Schumann with certain aspects of the symphony, although Schumann's lack of skill as writer for orchestra manifested itself in obvious flaws in the scoring. Performances by lighter-toned period instrument ensembles reveal a bit more clarity than those by the big late romantic orchestras, but few would put Schumann in a class with his contemporaries Wagner, Berlioz, or Mendelssohn, for that matter. Other well-known works Schumann started or finished around this time were the Piano Concerto and the Second and Fourth Symphonies.

The Schumann's first child, Marie, was born on September 1, 1841. Later that year, Clara traveled to Weimar to play duets in recital with Franz Liszt, another friend and admirer of Schumann's work. Balancing Clara's career with his became crucial, as she could earn a significant income and was also eager to perform. Early in 1842 Clara embarked on a tour of Denmark and northern Germany. Schumann, seemingly growing less and less sociable, came along for part of the trip. Following his normal pattern, the composer also embarked on a year of chamber music, writing several of the works for small ensembles that would remain among his most popular, of which the Piano Quintet in E-flat Major, Op. 44, is probably the favorite of most. Surging ahead on waves of joy at one moment then shadowed intriguingly the next, this seductive work is hard not to like. Also written in 1842, the Quartet for Piano and Strings, Op. 47, is pitched a bit lower, but still beautiful and no less worthwhile. Before these came the three string quartets (Op. 41). Lyrical, well made, and likable enough, Schumann's quartets break no ground in a form taken to dizzy heights by Haydn, Mozart, Beethoven, and sometimes Schubert.

In 1844 the Schumanns traveled to Russia on a tour for Clara that was financially rewarding as well as revealing about the difficulty she had traveling with her husband. She was at the time the more famous half of the couple, with the sensitive, taciturn Schumann often behaving oddly in social situations, leaving people to wonder whether anything was wrong with him. Fears kept him from climbing a famous tower in Saint Petersburg and from crossing the River Neva in a small boat. The tour was good financially for the Schumanns, though, and Clara was recognized as a major talent wherever she played, including a long performance in Saint Petersburg for the imperial family.

Back in Leipzig in 1845, Schumann worked on his Symphony No. 2, a problematic work that displays more than a few flashes of greatness and in which some profess to perceive early symptoms of the insanity that would overtake him eleven years later, as well as the Fantasy for Piano and Orchestra, the first version of what would become one of his most popular works, the A Minor Piano Concerto. Schumann's shift to more formal structures paralleled a neoclassical reaction in the musical world to the high romanticism of the 1830s, of which Schumann himself along with Chopin and Berlioz had been the chief practitioners. It's worth noting that the wildness of Berlioz's early music did eventually take on more classical proportions, although his later stylistic adjustments sound and fit better than Schumann's; Chopin continued stubbornly and gloriously along his chosen track as a writer for the piano alone.

Yet another physical, emotional, and spiritual crisis of Robert's persuaded the Schumanns to resettle in 1845 in Dresden, the capital of Saxony and another major German musical center. Usually pregnant during these years, Clara toured locally, helping the family's finances and securing her own reputation as a leading performer. In 1847 Schumann returned to chamber music, composing two of his three piano trios, of which the first, in D minor, speaks with appealing warmth and passion, if no longer the wildness and fire of the early period. In a bitter blow, their close friend Mendelssohn died in November of that year. As Mendelssohn had stood at the top of the German musical hierarchy, his advice and advocacy would be missed, along with his personal warmth. His death, did, however, open career opportunities for Schumann that the composer lacked the stability and temperament to exploit successfully.

In 1848, a year of political upheavals across Europe, the politically liberal couple watched with distress as reactionary governments indiscriminately racked up body counts among civilian protesters, with news spread swiftly by free press in most of the German states and impelled by new telegraphic technology. Schumann returned to the piano, writing the *Waldszenen*—"Forest Scenes"—Op. 82, and the *Album für die Jugend*—"Album for the Young"—Op. 68. Flashes of the young master can be heard in both sets, especially in "The Prophet Bird" from the former work, one of Schumann's weirdest conceptions from that or any period. The presence of an excellent choir in Dresden encouraged the composer to write works, now completely neglected, for a variety of vocal ensembles. Part of the dramatic cantata Scenes from Goethe's *Faust* and his setting of portions of Byron's *Manfred* come from the same era.

Many nonoperatic composers have hoped to write operas but found themselves stymied by the lack of a libretto—the text—they can work with. Brahms never found one; Ravel wrote two odd little operatic works; in the category of single producers are Beethoven, Debussy, and Schumann. *Genoveva*, the composer's single operatic work does not stand alongside *Fidelio* or *Pelléas et Mélisande* in reputation, nor is it likely to join those great one-offs. Mid-nineteenth-century arts had found in medieval legends, such as that of *Genoveva*, a marvelous source of subjects; but Schumann's undramatic temperament produced a work that has proven immune to revival since its premiere in 1850. Received eagerly because it came from the by-then-respected composer, the work's flaws were also evident from the start. It's interesting that this great writer of songs was unable to make his powerful skill at lyrical characterization work in the bigger arena of opera.

In 1850, Schumann was appointed municipal music director in Düsseldorf, a big city on the Rhine, far west across the then-fragmented German states from the cities and towns where the Schumanns had grown up and lived. The job was prestigious—Mendelssohn had once held it—but much too stressful and demanding for the hypersensitive and by then half-crazy Schumann. He gave it his all, though, creating and leading programs of noble and serious works, including the Passion settings of Bach, several Handel oratorios, the Schubert C-major Symphony he had discovered, Chopin's F Minor Piano Concerto and Mendelssohn's "Italian" Symphony. He also worked steadily on his own compositions, the best known of which is the Symphony No. 3, nicknamed "Rhenish." For this chunky, Germanic music (a bit ponderous for some) the composer finds an unusual but effective five-movement form. The extraordinarily productive Schumann wrote some of his largest pieces, many for chorus and orchestra, including the Mass, Op. 147, and the Requiem, Op. 148, at this time, as well as numerous choral and vocal settings, also well made but often curiously anonymous, too.

Before long the Düsseldorf authorities found out just how poor a choice for conductor the uncommunicative Schumann was. Often, Clara sat in on rehearsals, actively interpreting her husband's desires for the musicians and singers and playing the piano as they practiced choral works.[8] It was also while in Düsseldorf that the Schumanns were introduced to two younger musicians who would be among the most important of the second half of the nineteenth century: violinist Joseph Joachim and the twenty-year-old Johannes Brahms. Deeply impressed with the latter's genius, Schumann returned to journalism to praise him in print as a return to the fire and freedom of his own youth. For his part, as noted, Brahms saw in Schumann if not exactly a father, then a guide whose example he wanted to follow.

Relations between Düsseldorf authorities and the Schumanns deteriorated; as Robert's responsibilities were curtailed and he focused on the formalist works of his last few productive years. Some are performed; many aren't, but it's safe to say that they are as a group surprisingly bland and unmemorable, and, subjectively, difficult to love. The list includes a number of songs and chamber works, including the sonatas for violin and piano.

Robert and Clara made a successful tour to Rotterdam in December 1853, where she performed to appreciative audiences and he was hailed as a hero. But Schumann himself had been suffering increasingly from a variety of symptoms, including difficulties in hearing and speaking. Over the years he had occasionally heard a musical note when none was being played, and he found this auditory hallucination returning more often and with greater intensity. In mid-February 1854, the sounds became more ferocious and Schumann began to describe them in terms of demonic torment, while other, more beautiful imagined sounds were ascribed to angels. He became worried about injuring Clara or his children unintentionally, and although never religious before, began to talk about his torments as punishment for sinful deeds. Amid the madness were moments of clarity, including one where Schumann said he wanted to be committed to an asylum. But on the afternoon of February 27 Schumann slipped out of his house, got to the center of a bridge crossing the Rhine, climbed down (there were many witnesses, and he didn't "throw himself in" as many older biographies state) and stepped into the frigid water. He was rescued immediately by men in a fishing boat, whose aid he fought. In early March he was brought to the most liberal and enlightened mental hospital in western Germany, run by Dr. Franz Richarz, in the town of Endenich, near Bonn.

The history of Schumann's last two years is among the saddest of any composer's. Believing that Clara's presence would agitate Schumann, Richarz thought it best for her to stay away; she saw him only once, on July 27, 1856, when, though incoherent, he seemed to recognize her. He died two days later. No historian, medical or musical, knows for certain what killed Schumann. Once it's understood that every word on the subject is speculative, the most logical and sensible theory is that the syphilis he probably contracted at twenty returned in 1854 in its tertiary phase, attacking his nervous system. Although a common illness, its cause was not discovered until 1905, so there was no chance of Schumann's receiving effective treatment. Other symptoms, including the permanently dilated pupils of Schumann's eyes, lend credence to the syphilis theory.

Characterizing a man as troubled and talented as Schumann, whose psyche was a laundry list of neuroses, psychoses, and organic illnesses is a tall order. His fear of insanity was not unreasonable; psychic disturbances must have started early in his life. Some biographers who admire his music act as though little was wrong with him before 1854, when clearly there was plenty. Schumann's ability to function in the world seems to have diminished over the years, with Clara running interference, although his capacity to work remained with him even after he was committed to the hospital at Endenich.

Looking at Schumann's mind and character forces us to consider a number of factors, including the apparent bipolarity that allowed him when manic to work at a furious pace, explaining as well his depressions, panic attacks, phobias, and hypochondria. At a lower level of pathology is the composer as the obsessive-compulsive self-organizer, manager of domestic accounts and, with everyone's favorite Schumannesque obsession, noting in his diary with an *f* the occasions when he and Clara had sex, twice a week on average. This was also the side that became an obsessive object counter and list compiler within the asylum in his final two years. Yet he continued to work hard even as he suffered. Clara, a woman of accomplishment, high intelligence, and strong character seems to have loved him with few reservations or complaints. According to all accounts, Schumann doted on and played enthusiastically with his seven children; naturally the older ones, especially his first daughter, Marie, received more attention and love than did those born later. Mendelssohn, Brahms, and Joachim, formidable musicians, treated him with respect as a fellow professional and liked him as a friend.

Famous as a performer and revered as the composer's widow, Clara lived until 1896, remaining close with Brahms, who died the following year. Speculation that they became lovers remains unsubstantiated. Eugenie, the last of the Schumann children, survived until 1938. Since she was only three years old when her father was institutionalized, it's unlikely she remembered him at all.

3 The Works for Piano

The first twenty-three of Schumann's published compositions, written in the stormy years between 1832 and 1840, are for the piano. Among these stand some of his greatest and most popular works, including *Carnaval*, Op. 9; *Kinderszenen*, Op. 15; and the *Fantasie*, Op. 17. Some, like *Papillons*, Op. 2; *Davidsbündlertänze*, Op. 6; and the *Études symphoniques*, Op. 13, may be less familiar to newbies, but are in the same league. Others from this era are little known even to dedicated fans of the piano repertory, but as this was the composer's boldest and most imaginative phase, just about all of it is worth hearing.

The works fall into several formal categories. The most familiar are the suites of short (or shortish) character pieces, including *Papillons, Davidsbündlertänze, Carnaval, Kreisleriana*, Op. 16, and the *Humoreske*, Op. 20 all of which are tightly woven from start to finish and must be heard and understood in their entireties. The first three above form a subgroup, based on the idea of a dance suite, but given by Schumann new dimensions and deeper meanings. While close to these in its structure and unity of aesthetic, elements of the twelve-part *Kinderszenen* can be performed alone. With the *Fantasiestücke*, Op. 12, Schumann devised a slightly different formula where the individual elements are somewhat longer in duration and more independent in personality and structure, though they may be performed together, too. The *Noveletten*—"Novelettes"—Op. 21, *Nachtstücke*—"Night Pieces"—Op. 23, and the *Romanzen*—obviously, "Romances"—Op. 28, belong to this group. It's also the category the composer would employ when he returned to the piano later in his career. Several works, including the popular Toccata, Op. 7, and the *Arabeske*, Op. 18, are one-offs.

There are also three categories where Schumann works in more traditional forms. These include the three named sonatas, Opp. 11, 14, and 22, and the *Fantasie*, Op. 17, which is sonata-like and the greatest of the four. There are two sets of technical studies, Opp. 3 and 10, based on themes of the violin virtuoso and composer Niccolò Paganini. Finally, there are three sets of variations, of which Opp. 1 and 5 are both quite good. These are overshadowed by the mammoth *Études symphoniques*, an astonishing set of technical studies in variation form. (Variations state a theme at the beginning, then subject it to all manner of alterations. These works can range in dimension and ambition from short and trivial to huge and profound. The best known among the great sets for keyboard are Bach's *Goldberg Variations* and Beethoven's Variations on a Theme by Diabelli, Op. 120.)

Several external factors also cut across Schumann's early works for piano. The best known of these is his attribution of lively and energetic passages to his own self-created identity named "Florestan" and the more introspective ones to "Eusebius," another invented side of his creative personality. These are at their most exposed in the *Davidsbündlertänze*, and *Carnaval*, the energy and charm of which are generated to a great extent by the proximity and contrast between exuberance and melancholy. His Op. 1, the Variations on the Name "ABEGG," turns a musical pun into a quasi-literary one, as it's named for a made-up dedicatee. The *Fantasie* contains musical quotations from Beethoven, and *Kreisleriana* is founded on a reference to a character from fiction by E. T. A. Hoffmann. The title of the *Noveletten* also displays Schumann's inclination toward the literary.

A key responsibility of a survey is to clarify background and context. So, although unavoidable, the frequent explanations do seem to clog descriptions of the music. It's far more important to grasp that while complex, the music is mostly enjoyable and easy to appreciate without knowing anything about Florestan, Eusebius, or the fictional Pauline von Abegg.

Variations on the Name "ABEGG," Op. 1

The title requires a series of explanations that are typical of the composer's early style, with literary and musical gamesmanship at nearly the same high pitch. It's a fine, playful start to Schumann's career. The dedication to the nonexistent "Countess Pauline von Abegg" sets up a joke on the notes and the musical idea as well as the pun on the countess's name. Like some of his German predecessors, notably Bach, Schumann uses the names of the notes that in English are called C, D, E, F, G, A, B, which are the white keys on the piano, with their attendant sharps and flats—the black keys—to create the regular, lilting waltz on which this relatively short (seven-minute) but intriguing work is built (German speakers use B for B-flat, with H standing for B-natural).

As you may have figured out by now, theme consists of an arching five-note theme on the notes A, B-flat, E, G, and G that Schumann extends into a longer but still regular pattern. Bland in itself, the theme is brought to life a throbbing left hand accompaniment displaying the composer's irrepressible manic energy. The first of the five variations is elegant and quite difficult, requiring technical skill of a high order. In the second variation, Schumann passes the theme to the left hand, to which he gives the unusual instruction "*il Basso parlando*"—"the bass speaks." There's much syncopation, and the accompaniment throughout is a limping figure that's a good example of the strangeness of the composer's imagination. The third variation is a more standard affair, with whirring triplets (three notes squeezed into the space of two) in the right hand decorating a broken version of the theme in the left. In the fourth Schumann shifts the key daringly for a dreamy-sounding, lavishly decorated iteration not unlike a Chopin nocturne. The final variation, marked "*Finale alla Fantasia*"—"like a fantasy"—contains an unusual and in fact unplayable musical idea: the notes of the theme are struck in order, held a bit, then *released* with sharp accents, something no piano or pianist has even been capable of. Here, as we'll see often in his early works, ideas, some of them quite odd, behind the music are as important as the notes themselves. While no one can claim they reach great heights, the "ABEGG" Variations hold up well, displaying freshness and sophistication alongside the peculiarity that's entirely typical of early Schumann.

Papillons, Op. 2

One of Schumann's greatest and most characteristic works, *Papillons*—"Butterflies"—also sets the course for later achievements, notably the *Davidsbündlertänze* and *Carnaval*, the latter probably his most popular keyboard composition. Assembled from existing sketches and published in 1831, this strange little waltz suite takes Schubert's model to a new level, layering innocent dances with ironies and echoes that endow them with an altogether different range of expression (Schubert was entirely capable of depth and irony, he just didn't bother in his suites of short waltzes and German dances). *Papillons* is also the first composition in which Schumann depicts memory and time through music, returning to the first dance as an echo toward the end. It's a stunning effect, and one that the composer will deploy with equal skill and over longer time spans in *Davidsbündlertänze* and *Carnaval*.

A typical nineteenth-century waltz suite alternates fiery with more lyrical dances, as Schumann does in *Papillons*. Chopin's individual waltzes are all actually small suites containing several dances of contrasting character. In several, Chopin adds artifice and irony by, for example, opening one with a passage giving the listener the sense of approaching the ballroom. Another fine example of imaginative treatment of what was once a familiar, even hackneyed idea of a suite of waltzes is Carl Maria von Weber's *Invitation to the Dance*, composed in 1819 and surely familiar to Schumann. Once enormously popular, *Invitation* frames the dances within opening and closing passages of great charm imitating musically the polite conversation of a man and woman attending the ball.

What sets Schumann apart from everyone else is that the sense of contrast normal to a waltz set is brought to a new level well described as fragmentation by one commentator.[1] This the composer accomplishes by various means, including keeping the dances short, contrast between the changes of tonality (of key) that go beyond the norm, as well as the standard approach of alternating the character of the dances in the sequence. Sometimes he even darts away from his ideas within each tiny dance.

Following a seconds-long introduction in an expectant mood, the first waltz, its rising, sighing, and fluttering tune that will be familiar to anyone who has heard *Carnaval*, where it briefly reappears, passes. The second is in a key that's a radical leap from the first; the third is a stamping country dance, its deliberate crudity differing from anything else in the work. Immediately memorable, the fourth has a lilting delicacy. I'm only describing these because they give you an idea about the character of *Papillons*; it's not a hard work to listen to or grasp. Be aware as you listen that most of the dances are in two parts, with the second contrasting sometimes radically with the first, all contributing to that sense of fragmentation that carries the work. The eleventh dance is the longest and contains the most diverse thematic material and abrupt shifts. If you've seen or heard Tchaikovsky's *Nutcracker*, then you may know the tune that opens the twelfth dance; known as the "Grandfather's Dance," it was a signal from the band that a ball was ending. Already old when Schumann quoted it here, it evokes older, perhaps better times. The sighing first waltz returns first nostalgically, then combined movingly with the "Grandfather's Dance." Six notes imitate a clock chime; notes stretch out and the volume drops. Schumann ends the work on a quiet but energetic three-note bump in the bass.

Paganini Studies, Op. 3
Intermezzi, Op. 4
Impromptus on a Theme of Clara Wieck, Op. 5

These three early compositions are infrequently performed, but all are works of real if varying merit. Charged with an energy late Schumann lacks, audiences might enjoy hearing them from time to time. All three are extremely difficult.

The Paganini Studies are adaptations for the keyboard of six short compositions by Niccolò Paganini (1782–1840), the seminal violin virtuoso whose playing hypnotized and staggered those who heard him perform. The second, in E major, based on a musical depiction of a hunt, with echoing horns wittily imitated, was also adapted skillfully by Liszt, whose lighter touch seems better to capture the spirit of the original. Although a great deal of effort for a performer, Schumann's six are enjoyable and well worth hearing.

More ambitious in scope, the six Intermezzi anticipate *Kreisleriana* without achieving the sustained brilliance or structural cohesion of the later work. They suffer from Schumann's typical shortcoming of sitting on his ideas for too long and repeating them too often. That said, many of those ideas are strong and daring. The Intermezzi could also benefit from occasional revival.

The Impromptus on a Theme of Clara Wieck are (obviously) based on a tender theme by the young pianist-composer who would become the composer's wife. Like Opp. 3 and 4, the Impromptus have had little traction with pianists or audiences. In fact, they are a lively and interesting set of variations on Wieck's theme. Schumann skillfully controls the sense of expansion from the gravity of the theme through brightening textures and movement of the first six variations. In the fifth he experiments to little audible effect with the hands playing in different meters; in the disturbing final section of *Kreisleriana* Schumann will show full mastery of that technique. On the negative side, the final variation is too long as the composer gets bogged down in a quasi-fugal passage that shows his weakness in counterpoint, the note-against-note compositional technique brought to its highest level by Bach.

Davidsbündlertänze, Op. 6

As mentioned earlier, the Germanic mouthful of a title means "Dances of the Band of David," Schumann's imaginary society of musical anti-Philistines. He composed it in 1837, then revised it for the worse in 1850, adding repeats and otherwise tampering with the daring and momentum of this astonishing work. Matthias Zimmermann's excellent performance on the CD at the back of the book is of the later version. Recordings of the first edition are inexplicably rare, but there's one by the great Italian pianist Maurizio Pollini you'll also want to hear. Schumann's initial identifies each of the movement's identities within his mental cast of characters (Florestan, Eusebius, or both) and features two stage direction–like comments that Schumann also removed from the 1850 revision. These are so strikingly indicative of the composer's early manner that I have included them in the descriptions of the eighteen sections that follow.

Closer than a cousin, *Carnaval* is more like its nonidentical twin. With its twenty-one humorous movements that flash by and a closing passage that's far more brilliant, *Carnaval* has, perhaps understandably, always been more popular. If you like *Carnaval* but haven't heard *Davidsbündlertänze*, perhaps put off by the spiky name, then you're almost sure to appreciate the latter, because it's every bit as good. More wild, passionate, profound, moody, elliptical and with even greater contrasts among the eighteen character pieces that make it up, *Davidsbündlertänze* remains a bit of a sleeper in Schumann's oeuvre, though its popularity seems to have gained over the years—as well it should.

As noted, each dance carries a postscript, assigning its genesis to the lively and impetuous Florestan or the reflective Eusebius. These sides of Schumann's bipolar mind reflect the mood (or moods) of each of the eighteen character pieces. Some (numbers 1, 13, 15 and 17) contain impetuous and lyrical passages and are credited to both characters. Two (numbers 9 and 18, at the work's midpoint and end) also have stage directions, an unusual and perhaps singular procedure. Again, you should find *Davidsbündlertänze* readily enjoyable without worrying about any of this, in part because you'll easily sense the difference in moods as you listen. They're included because they were so important to Schumann himself in writing the work.

1. (CD Track 1). The first dance opens with a leaping figure in the left hand, identified as "Motto von C.W." who is Clara Wieck, a fragment borrowed from a short dance by Clara. The bulk of the first dance consists of a long-limbed waltz with phrases that alternately rise and fall. Schumann assigns it to both Florestan and Eusebius.
2. (Track 2) The second dance, another waltz with a sweetly harmonized, winding theme, is deeply melancholy. It returns toward the end of the work to great effect. (Eusebius)

3. (Track 3) The exuberant third dance, given the expression mark "With humor," opens with a leaping, technically difficult figure for both hands, followed by a breathless, syncopated passage of high energy. It ends, like several other numbers, with a more fluid, lighter-textured closing passage. (Florestan)
4. (Track 4) Schumann marks this high-energy and -velocity study in syncopation to be played "with impatience." (Florestan)
5. (Track 5) The fifth piece is more of a tender aria than a dance. (Eusebius)
6. (Track 6) One of the most interesting tempo and expressive indications in the work stood in the 1837 version at the start of this thick textured, syncopated, seething tarantella: "Very fast and within itself [i.e., repressed]."[2] The composer later cut the marking to a straightforward "Very fast," omitting its psychological side. As with number three, there's a lighter but still intense coda, or closing passage. (Florestan)
7. (Track 7) Like No. 5 not really a dance, this meditation revolves slowly over rolled chords and hovering melodic phrases that float asymmetrically away. It also displays a detachment unlike any of the eighteen; and takes on ever greater meaning as one gets to know the *Davidsbündlertänze.* (Eusebius)
8. (Track 8) Another study in syncopation, this spiky and impatient passage flashes by in seconds, contrasting as strongly as it can with No. 7. Schumann displays admirable flexibility in phrasing here too. (Florestan)
9. (Track 9) Overflowing with feeling, the main tune of this central panel is set in a repeated long-short rhythm over a choppy left-hand accompaniment. At its head is the phrase "Hereupon Florestan stopped, and his lips trembled sorrowfully."[3]
10. (Track 10) The second half of the *Davidsbündlertänze* opens with a rolling proto-Brahmsian ballade where the composer shifts the melody, alternately thunderous and beseeching, from the deep in the bass to the right hand. (Florestan)
11. (Track 11) More song than dance, this long-breathed melody expands into extended, irregular phrases. (Eusebius)

12. (Track 12) A leaping, whirling, fantastical figure in the right hand spins over a bumping accompaniment in the left. The composer's expression indication is "with humor." (Florestan)
13. (Track 13) Thick chords play a fiercely joyous short-short-long idea that ends in a shout of triumph. In the middle section, tolling notes in the left hand accompany a calmer idea in the right. Schumann ends this, the work's wildest movement with another fluid, light footed coda. (Florestan and Eusebius)
14. (Track 14) Another aria rather than a dance, here a sweet melody floats over rolling arpeggios. (Eusebius)
15. (Track 15) A volcanic and triumphant chord sequence that's very hard to play is followed by a rapturous melody spun out over and under rapid arpeggios. (Florestan and Eusebius)
16. (Track 16) Marked to be played "with good humor," this difficult study in syncopated chords turns menacing with strange eruptions. It doesn't end but instead melts into:
17. (Track 17) A slower, quieter section in which horn calls and chimes are suggested as from a distance. Then, in the masterstroke of *Davidsbündlertänze*, Schumann unexpectedly brings back the sad waltz from No. 2, to devastating effect, showing him capable of long-range thinking, demonstrating why he can't be pigeonholed as a miniaturist. An accelerating choreographic passage brings the piece to a close on a rising chord sequence of breathtaking beauty.
18. (Track 18) The final dance seems as though it's tacked on. Schumann's stage direction is: "Quite redundantly, Eusebius added the following; but great happiness shone in his eyes the while."[4] The tiny waltz seems to smile through tears, before ending this great and daring work on notes tolling quietly in the piano's lowest register.

Toccata, Op.7

If you've listened to the keyboard music of Bach, you may be familiar with this title. It's a generic name for a piece designed to show off a player's touch (*tocca* in Italian) on a keyboard instrument. Conceived when he was only eighteen, Schumann revised it over several years, finally publishing the work in 1834. A showpiece of legendary difficulty, the Toccata demonstrates the composer's preoccupation with technique at this early phase in his career; his own skills must have been formidable to invent something so hard. And yet the Toccata is playful and even amusing in spots, with Schumann firmly in control of its structure.

The work is in sonata form, meaning that it's cast in three big sections, the first (the exposition) where themes are presented, followed by the development, where they are played off each other, then ending in the recapitulation where the themes are reviewed. Here, as often with sonata movements, there's also a closing section called a coda. So, although Schumann captures the virtuosic idea of the baroque title, his Toccata is firmly classical in form. The syncopated swagger of the chords that open the work capture one's attention, as does the rattling activity that follows. Typically for Schumann, and fittingly for a toccata, some of the material has a manic giddiness. Almost every technical difficulty is thrown at the player, with repeated notes and murderous runs in double notes as notable challenges. The coda opens with furious hammered notes, settles down a bit with repeated iterations of one of the calmer themes, then ends in five noble chords.

Allegro in B Minor, Op. 8

The first movement of an uncompleted sonata, Schumann published this rarely heard fragment in 1835. Like the Toccata, it's in three-part form, with contrasting ideas and a fair bit of experimentation as the composer tries to build difficult passagework into the sonata structure. Imperfect but impressive in its way, the Allegro could benefit from more frequent performance.

Carnaval, Op. 9

Certainly Schumann's most popular work, *Carnaval* is in every way suited for success. Unlike its sibling *Davidsbündlertänze*, its title is straightforward, requiring no translation or complicated explanations.

Its construction, with the character pieces that make it up distributed is flawless, and the return in the headlong final section of ideas from the opening is accomplished with incomparable skill. The tone of this most outgoing of Schumann's works is playful and often downright cheerful, without the mood swings of *Davidsbündlertänze*. The pieces are short, forestalling boredom. In *Carnaval* the composer never seems to take on the burden of profundity, skating wittily across the surfaces he creates, but paradoxically the work is substantial and deeply satisfying.

Like the "ABEGG" Variations, *Carnaval* is constructed partially on a play of notes. (Its subtitle is *Scènes mignonnes sur quatre notes*—"Charming scenes on four notes"; the French names and references are in the language that was shared by educated nineteenth-century Europeans of many nationalities.) Again, no one's enjoyment in listening has been diminished by ignorance of this background, which I'll explain briefly as it appears in the titles of the pieces. Each of the twenty-one character pieces has a title, some generic, some drawn from Schumann's fantasy world, and two remarkable sketches honoring contemporary musicians he admired.

1. *Préambule.* Schumann endows the proclamatory chord sequence with high energy, making it memorable with slight shifts in emphasis in each of its widening iterations. This leads to a headlong passage over continual rhythmic hiccups, followed by a flitting idea that's the first of many with that profile in *Carnaval.* Another rushing idea that will return leads to one last, breathless melodic phrase.
2. *Pierrot.* Named for a clownish figure from the once popular commedia dell'arte theatrical tradition, a steady chord sequence is interrupted continually by a falling three-note phrase in a short-short-long rhythm.
3. *Arlequin.* Another commedia dell'arte reference. Unlike its predecessor, this flitting waltz sparkles. There's also a falling figure, this one gracefully embedded in the tune.
4. *Valse noble.* A broadly phrased, slow waltz with a contrasting middle section.

5. *Eusebius.* Schumann's meditative identity is represented by a slow, twisting melody in two forms, the first long-breathed, the second slightly compressed.
6. *Florestan.* The composer's impetuous side is well represented in a surging waltz marked "*passionato.*" As though in a dream, the plaintive rising opening waltz from *Papillons* floats by before an agitated return to the passionate waltz.
7. *Coquette*—"Flirt"—is translated into a flitting figure. This merges with
8. *Réplique*—"Reply"—in which mellow and presumably masculine five-note phrase responds to the flirting. These two sections resemble in a general way the opening and closing passages of Weber's *Invitation to the Dance.* "Sphinxes," which follows in the score, shows the musical puzzle behind *Carnaval*, but it's not meant to be played.
9. *Papillons*, which as we know means "butterflies," is a fast country dance with a busy middle section.
10. *A.S.C.H—S.C.H.A* (*Lettres dansantes*)—"Dancing Letters." Four of the notes of the musical puzzle are named in another light-textured, flitting waltz.
11. *Chiarina* is Schumann's nickname for Clara, here depicted in a fine and fiery waltz.
12. *Chopin* expresses Schumann's admiration for the style and skill of his contemporary. The imitation of the Polish composer's nocturnal manner, with a long-limbed melody over sweeping arpeggios, is warmhearted and sharply observed.
13. *Estrella*, like *Chiarina* a few moments earlier, a waltz with a sharp profile, is a tribute to Ernestine von Fricken, Schumann's one-time fiancée.
14. *Reconnaissance.* The French word has several related meanings, but the central sense is that of recognition. This delicate study in keyboard techniques is one of the longer in *Carnaval* and one that many find among its most memorable. A warm melody floats over detached repeated notes and a rocking accompaniment in the outer sections, with the accompaniment syncopated in the central part.
15. *Pantalon et Colombine*—the names of another two characters out of the commedia dell'arte. The outer sections of this fast tempo

movement represent the frantic Pantalon in detached notes and sharp chords. The middle section treats the melody smoothly and in more mellow harmony.

16. *Valse allemande*—"German Waltz"—features a comically phrased melody (very short–very long) followed by a deliberately stodgy chord sequence. It's interrupted by
17. *Paganini* (*Intermezzo*) is another witty tribute to the great violinist and his mesmerizing playing. This ends in thunderous, un-violin-like chords deep in the keyboard before returning to the "Valse allemande," which then flits blandly along as though nothing had happened.
18. *Aveu*—"Vow" a brief movement containing delicate but impassioned melody.
19. *Promenade*. Somewhat like the *Valse noble*, the phrases of this grand and nostalgic dance rise and fall with the ease and regularity of breathing.
20. *Pause*. Only seconds long, this propulsive passage brought back from the *Préambule* serves as a lead-in to the finale.
21. The concluding *Marche des "Davidsbündler" contre les Philistins*—"March of the Band of David Against the Philistines"—opens with a grandiose but playful march set by Schumann in three-quarter time, rather than the normal four-beat rhythm. The composer brings back thematic material from the *Préambule*, including the flitting theme and many entertaining rhythmic hiccups. In the left hand, the old "Grandfather's Dance" is hammered out powerfully. Ideas seem to fly by ever more dizzyingly, as phrases from earlier are roared out in an ending wild with excitement, humor, and joy.

Six Concert Studies on Caprices by Paganini, Op. 10

The composer's preoccupation with the Italian violin master continued after the Op. 3 studies also based on material by Paganini. The brilliant sketch named for Paganini in *Carnaval* is, as we've seen, a funny but loving tribute rather than a literal transcription. Like Op. 3, these substantial works are rarely performed but of genuine merit, as Schumann does justice to the charm of Paganini's melodic ideas. The thickly written keyboard textures don't really translate the brilliant sound of the violin, so unlike that of the piano. As before, Liszt's reinterpretations are lighter, more rhythmically incisive, and capture more of their virtuoso swagger. But these are impressive in their way, and well worth hearing.

Sonata No. 1 in F-sharp Minor, Op. 11

Although not his first run at the formal icon of the sonata, this was the first Schumann completed and published. This ambitious but flawed piece puts the composer's strengths and weaknesses on full display. Dedicated to "Fräulein Clara Wieck," the sonata overflows with passion and beautiful, rhapsodic material. Its shortcomings stem from Schumann's inability or unwillingness to make them fit into sonata form, or perhaps to apply its rules to the wrong kind of material. Also, in the first and last movements, the composer falls into a dangerous pattern of repeating one rhythmic figure "almost obsessively."[5] Be that as it may, the Sonata No. 1 is easy to like, warts and all. It's a noble effort that's too rich to consider a failure.

The very long first movement is as noted a procession of beautiful ideas, starting with a smoldering introductory passage with a sharply accented theme set over rolling triplets. The main thematic idea has a Spanish snap, and is the one that Schumann flogs relentlessly. It builds however into a climactic phrase that overflows with passion. The composer finds himself hard pressed to set these ideas, all highly individual, into the interplay that sonata form demands. He feels responsible to go through the motions of recapitulating, even though the material doesn't need to be repeated. The second movement, titled *Aria*, is a simple three-part lyrical statement. The opening theme, shared between the hands over a pulsing accompaniment is very beautiful, as is the more flowing middle section. Here, Schumann's restraint in setting his material out without excess is admirable, as the movement lasts only about three and one-half minutes. His brevity here throws the gargantuan proportions of the opening movement into relief.

Titled *Scherzo ed Intermezzo* (*scherzo* is Italian for "joke"), the daring third movement may be the most successful of the composer's experiments in this sonata. Its influence on Brahms is obvious, from the opening section with its flood of rhythmically charged ideas that skip, roll, and hop. The middle part (the "intermezzo") contains another profusion of ideas, these of trademark Schumannesque peculiarity and boldness. One is like a recitative, a speechlike form of vocal music; it's reminiscent of a famous passage from the finale of Beethoven's Symphony No. 9. One has to wonder what it's doing here, but everything flashes by with admirable speed.

Like the opening movement, the finale is too long, poorly organized, and set into obsessive rhythmic patterns. But it also overflows with magnificent ideas, from the thunderous chords at the opening to the two completely discrete skipping themes (the first brusque, the next dreamy) that follow without transition. There's another, completely different chordal eruption, a pair of swaying, propulsive ideas that could have come from *Carnaval*, and a still, folklike melody of high profile. It's a wild but gorgeous mess.

Fantasiestücke, Op. 12

Unlike the great suites of character pieces, the eight "Fantasy Pieces" are neither linked, fragmentary, or absolutely inseparable. Only the final piece carries a valedictory burden, needing what came before to make complete sense. As such, they're the first of several sets for piano by Schumann of similar dimension and structure. They're longer, too, with each lasting three or four minutes. They are solid pieces, mostly of high quality, and technically difficult, particularly the fourth (*In der Nacht*) and seventh (*Traumes-Wirren*). With these eight the listener can sense movement in the composer's purpose away from virtuosity for its own sake toward a goal of more intense expressivity.

- Schumann opens the set with the best of the eight, *Des Abends*—"Evening." A marvel of delicacy and restraint, this sketch consists of a single gentle melody that merges with its accompaniment. Unlike most of the *Fantasiestücke*, it's based on one theme put through a few mild permutations in phrasing and rhythm; with dusty, twilit harmonies creating its most telling effects. It's also light in texture and transparent for Schumann, and the only of the *Fantasiestücke* with that quality.

- *Aufschwung*—"Soaring"—blends anxiety with exaltation. The piece opens with a short but rhythmically potent idea that captures a nightmarish dread with remarkable accuracy and can't help but remind one of Schumann's own anxieties. This is followed by an ecstatic idea, also memorable and fine. The contrasting middle section consists of quieter chords over a rolling accompaniment.
- *Warum?*—"Why?"—is the slowest and most frankly lyrical of the *Fantasiestücke*, little more than a statement of a rising melody over a pulsing and richly harmonized chord sequence.
- *Grillen*—"Whims"—is a good-natured, chunky chord study in a three-part setting. The composer's marking at the head is "with humor"; the performer should take the hint, as the chords sound better when taken with a light touch. The middle section, also chordal, would be solemn if not for the composer's rhythmic playfulness.
- *In der Nacht*—"In the Night"—is the most passionate element of the set and one of the best. Built of rushing arpeggios, chords broken into flowing—here rushing—figuration in the left hand, accompany a theme that's more cry than melody in the right. In the middle section the composer slows down and clouds the harmony to accompany a more complete but still dreamlike melody; under all the outcry of the opening section bubbles up nightmarishly. Rounding out the work, the opening section returns in abbreviated form.
- *Fabel*—"Fable"—is a witty musical narrative in which Schumann depicts an adult recounting a fairy tale to an excited child or children. The music is in three clearly demarked groups. In the opening the adult tale spinner can be heard summoning the kids and saying, "Once upon a time." Then in a remarkable example of musical mimesis, Schumann depicts the children's excitement in leaping figuration. The third element is the tale itself, depicted with mock drama in minor key tones and scales in sequences as the hero performs

brave deeds. The children are thrilled, and the adult's calm themes close this clever sketch, which could have come from or fit easily into the contemporaneous *Kinderszenen* or the *Noveletten.*

- *Traumes-Wirren*—"Dreams-Visions," a strange title, captures some of the manic excitement of the music, which opens with a giddy spinning idea that seems ready to fly off the rails. The middle section is a calmer chord sequence. It may be too much to read into *Traumes-Wirren*, but knowing Schumann's psychological difficulties makes this work more disturbing than its companions.
- *Ende vom Lied*—"The Story's End"—is the weakest of the set, opening with sequences of chunky chords that by this point seem overly hearty. Its moment of triumph sounds perfunctory; a bit like *Carnaval*'s but without that work's rhythmic energy.

Études symphoniques, Op.13

This sweeping set of variations on a theme "by an amateur" has an undeniable appeal. It's also a difficult but effective and musically substantial showpiece for a well-equipped pianist. With these obvious qualities, the work also contains two flaws, one major, the second at a subtle textural level. The bigger problem comes in the final section, a march of triumph that's too long, loud, and lacking subtlety. The lesser, albeit more pervasive problem stems from a lack of variety in phrasing, deriving from the theme itself. Schumann is far from alone among important composers in allowing the four-bar phrase to rule, putting the work into a predictable pattern that can become tiresome.

The curious title fails to call what's clearly a set of variations by name. The reason is that Schumann wanted to build it as a set of technical challenges, known (in French) as *études*—studies. The most famous nineteenth-century virtuoso piano studies are Chopin's, and Schumann's intention was to emphasize in the title the work's virtuosic character. A look at the score shows the individual pieces, of which there are nine from the original 1834 work, and five added in 1852, described as both etudes and variations and indeed the *Études symphoniques* is a dual work. The descriptor "symphonic" highlights its rich textures that strike toward an orchestral sound. Sharing an ambitious virtuosity with the suites of character pieces, the *Études* differs from them in its deeply serious posture.

The fact that there are earlier and later elements allows pianists to assemble the fifteen as they choose, with some alternating of the most difficult and tiring ones with others that allow for a bit of relaxation. The liner notes for a 1968 recording of the *Études* by the great pianist Sviatoslav Richter suggest that the five later variations are often inserted in between the fifth and sixth of the original set, as Richter does. While it's questionable whether that is really common practice, it does at least allow for a way of discussing them in a consistent sequence, so that's the order we'll follow. All regrettably confusing, but this important work deserves close examination.

The theme, curiously, is not Schumann's own but instead by Baron I. F. von Fricken, the adopted father of Ernestine, to whom Schumann was briefly engaged. It's a noble idea by that carries this great work, with the flaw mentioned above of overly regular phrasing as it falls and rises. This minor defect is magnified by the repetitious nature of the variation form. The first variation opens with the theme rendered in an energetic springing rhythm in the left hand, followed by a richly harmonized passage. Passionate and heaven-storming, the second variation moves the theme between the hands below and above chattering chords in the center of the keyboard. The very beautiful third sounds like another Paganini tribute, as Schumann makes the right hand imitate a violin in its fast arpeggios that accompany the theme in the left. Next comes a march in big, fierce chords. Then, the composer recasts the theme into a skipping rhythm.

Now we'll move with Richter to the five in the appendix. In these, all slow in tempo, the composer spreads out, finding more freedom here than in many of the original set. The first puts the theme into the left hand under rolling figuration in the right. The second and perhaps the best of these involves much hand crossing. Opening with compressed versions of the theme in the treble then the bass over murmured chords before spilling into a strange muttering incarnation, this marvelous passage navigates an expressive frontier between drama, lyricism, and rapture. In the third, Schumann compresses the rhythm of the theme to a waltzlike idea backed by rich harmony. The fourth of these later variations breaks the idea into another limping dance rhythm. The most openly lyrical of the work, the fifth moves to a major key melding theme and accompaniment into a relaxed and extended lyrical iteration not unlike a Chopin nocturne in sound and keyboard texture.

Returning to the original group, the (original) sixth sets the theme into tumbling wavelike figuration, and the seventh consists of slashing chords interspersed with grinding figuration. For the eighth, the composer parodies a stately baroque form known as a French overture, used a number of times by Bach. Schumann's reinterpretation here is manifestly strange. Next is a quick-tempo, notoriously difficult study in scampering chords, ending with a far-flung, spectral arpeggio. The tenth variation sets the theme in quick chords in the right hand over running figuration in the left.

The mysterious penultimate variation is a favorite of everyone who knows the *Études symphoniques.* Schumann recasts the theme into an irregular serpentine form against a murky and dissonant left-hand accompaniment. He then has a parallel thematic voice enter as the two melt together to a strange but magical harmonic effect known as suspension. The finale, completely different in mood and effect than anything before, is a march of triumph. Set in three parts, with the outer sections loud and heroic, and the middle a bit (but only a bit) quieter. The final page is enormously excited, with a manic, almost violent closing. In my opinion—which is not universal—this final variation is too long, too loud, repetitious, and stuck in its rhythmic grooves, both of which are hammered at mercilessly. Its points could be made more effectively if the material were shortened by a minute or two. With all respect to Schumann—and the *Études* certainly stands as one of his greatest achievements—he didn't always know when to quit. But to be clear: although the *Études symphoniques* has its flaws, it's a masterpiece.

Sonata No. 2 in F Minor, Op. 14

Nicknamed "Concerto Without Orchestra" by its publisher, Schumann's second published piano sonata has much in common with its predecessor.

It's loosely organized, murderously difficult, and uneven, with thrilling and commonplace ideas crowding side by side. Like many of this composer's works, it also has several versions, the most frequently performed having four movements. That's the one we'll discuss here.

The work opens with a thunderous falling figure in the bass followed by swirling figuration out of which a chain of passionate ideas emerge. An energetic skipping idea is the second subject. The dominant moods of the movement are pathos and passionate yearning. The second movement scherzo that follows is also serious rather than playful, it shifts often into strange rhythmic and harmonic patterns. Set in three parts, the outer sections are filled with a skipping idea and chunky chord sequences like some of the *Fantasiestücke*, these surrounding a middle section based on a broad melody.

The only section that contrasts with overflowing feel of the rest of the sonata, the contained third movements is a series of variations on a little funeral march by Clara Wieck. Filled with passionate outbursts and richly harmonized, the fourth variation is the most memorable, but the entire movement hangs together well. The composer unrealistically instructs that the finale be played *prestissimo possible*—as fast as possible—then asks for further accelerations; its boiling textures closely resemble the opening section of the contemporaneous *Kreisleriana.* While the pace of this wild but impressive movement never flags, a few long-limbed tunes find their way in. There are a couple of good recordings of the F Minor Sonata, but if the work intrigues you, make sure to hear the 1979 revival by Vladimir Horowitz.

Kinderszenen, Op. 15

"Scenes from Childhood" is one Schumann's most beloved works, and for good reason, as its thirteen short character pieces sketch childhood moods with penetrating imagination and skill. They show Schumann's gifts, here as an unabashed miniaturist, at their best. The composer steers clear of sentimentality because the works are clearly impressions and reflections of a mature mind on states of childhood. They're musically satisfying and much easier to play than anything before, explaining why many piano students learn them, and why you might have heard several apart from the sequence. The two most famous in the set are probably the opening number, "From Foreign Lands and People," and the seventh, "Daydreams." The former may be familiar from a sluggish and unsteady rendition in the 1979 Australian film *My Brilliant Career*; "Daydreams" was a staple encore of Horowitz's.

Most of the *Kinderszenen* are set simply, in two parts, with the longest ("Daydreams") occupying only two and one-half minutes' playing time. The opening piece, "From Foreign Lands and People," sets the mood with a lilting but thoughtful melody that passes from the right hand to the left. "Curious Story" opens with a cheerful phrase in a brisk rhythm, the second part featuring a winding melody. In "Tag," quick detached notes depict the children's darting steps. A regular rise and fall of phrase captures the sense of a murmured, carefully memorized prayer in "Praying Child." "Happy Enough" is the title of the sixth, expressing simple bliss in a melody that's sweet but never saccharine. Loud chords express excitement in "Important Event," the sixth of the set. "Daydreams" will be familiar to many. Its winding, irregularly phrased melody is richly harmonized; the composer captures the mystery of childhood without a sugar coating.

The eighth piece, "By the Fireside," suggests domestic bliss and busyness in another asymmetrical melody with a charming closing passage. One of the clearest examples of tone painting in *Kinderszenen*, "Knight of the Hobby-horse" displays the rocking rhythm of the toy and the uncontrolled excitement of the rider. In "Almost Too Serious," Schumann uses a long, articulate phrase to capture a different, thoughtful affect. Another group of moods and sensations including the shivers is well depicted in "Frightening," a sequence of varied ideas tied together with great skill. "Child Falling Asleep" is a lullaby that's at once tender but cool, as though viewed from the outside. The final section, "The Poet Speaks," is a nobly reflective chord sequence interspersed with more flowing material that must have sprung from the composer's improvisations.

Kreisleriana, Op. 16

The title refers to Johannes Kreisler, a fictional musician from E. T. A. Hoffmann's novel *Kater Murr* which runs on the conceit of alternating diary entries from Kreisler and his cat, who also keeps a journal, thus allowing for ironic observations by both. Immensely popular and influential in the nineteenth and early twentieth centuries, Hoffmann's works, like those of Edgar Allan Poe, focus on the uncanny and spectral. This was also an era when folktales (like those collected by the Grimm brothers) and folk music were regarded with new respect for their power and dreamlike strangeness.

Schumann's masterwork presents musical ideas of radically alternating character in eight densely packed sections, with each movement distinctly different from those around it. All eight contain at least one contrasting interlude as well, lending to the work a sense of pervasive unrest. Here the average playing time of each section is three to four minutes, longer than in the other character suites, but as with *Papillons*, *Davidsbündlertänze*, and *Carnaval*, there's no excerpting or tinkering with the composer's structure: the success of the whole hangs on the contrast between the sections and the carefully considered flow from start to finish. The overall moods of *Kreisleriana* are mystery, menace, and a demonic energy, broken by moments of lyrical reflection. *Kreisleriana* has many spiritual cousins in European music of the era, including the *Symphonie fantastique* of Berlioz and Wagner's *Der fliegende Holländer*—"The Flying Dutchman." In these, morbid and strange scenarios are treated seriously and with irresistible musical force. *Kreisleriana* has no story, but it's cut from the same cloth. Written seventy years later, Ravel's piano suite *Gaspard de la nuit* is another virtuoso exercise in musical demonism.

Kreisleriana is hard to play, if not quite at the level of *Gaspard* in terms of difficulty. Schumann poured his youthful powers, then at their height, into its dense textures, melodic richness and rhythmic drive. Folklike melodies can be heard in the slow fourth and sixth sections, and ideas with an improvisatory feel occur throughout. The final part contains a rhythmic game that's at once amusing and unnerving. *Kreisleriana* is one of Schumann's greatest achievements, and a musical companion for a lifetime, but it takes time to get to know. As with other art at this level, one never really gets to the bottom.

Expression of madness was one of the composer's goals in composing *Kreisleriana*, but as we've seen he came to fear the idea for himself, as he also grew less daring musically. As with the *Davidsbündlertänze*, Schumann revised the work in 1850, slowing what rushed ahead by adding repeats, regularizing many irregularities, and otherwise draining away much of its wildness and originality. So, as with *Davidsbündlertänze*, you'll want to seek out recordings of the first edition; again, Pollini (on Deutsche Grammophon) performs it well.

Schumann opens *Kreisleriana* at full boil, as the material seems to overspill the margins of expression. The first section consists of surging triplets in the right hand over off-the-beat chords in the left, expressing agitation and rage. This idea, which obsessed Schumann, would recur throughout his career. The middle section presents a lilting melody riding on a more delicate but still fluid accompaniment. Longest in the suite, the five-part second section opens with a generously proportioned archlike melody with a yearning affect. The first of two interludes consists of chiming chords over choppy sixteenth notes. After a leisurely restatement of the opening idea, the second intermezzo presents a forceful, sharply accented idea that incorporates sweeping arpeggios. The composer ends the section with an extended, quasi-improvisational fantasy on the arching tune.

Rather like the opening, the third section presents a driving theme punctuated by a four-note figure, but here Schumann reins in the rhythm, pushing the material ahead more purposefully. The extensive contrasting middle passage consists of an eloquent melodic idea that rises and falls. Equally interesting and effective is its galloping coda. The first of *Kreisleriana*'s two slow sections is a meditation that opens as if in midphrase. Textures are heavy, with melody and decoration placed deep into the bass, but the feeling evoked is profound. A rich melody over flowing broken chords marks the contrasting central panel. The composer brings back the opening phrase in abbreviated form to end the section.

A demonic but light-footed dance that twirls, skips, and hops opens the fifth section, with more extended melodic ideas following. Moving at the same speed, the central interlude starts with a fervently chanted idea before opening out into swirling figuration. In character much like the fourth section, the sixth opens with a gently exhaled melody with a folklike tint. More animated, the interlude expands warmly on a lilting idea from the opening phrase. As in the fourth section, the composer plumbs the depths here.

Probably the weakest part of *Kreisleriana*, the seventh section has several flaws. Although fiery, the opening passage is foursquare; the middle section consists of a trite harmonic progression[6] followed by a busy fugal idea that goes nowhere. But the calm chord sequence that closes it is inspired, and certainly everything moves along briskly, effectively setting up the devastating final movement.

Note, when you listen to *Kreisleriana*'s eighth and final part, how the left hand, which enters almost immediately after the sinister skipping theme in the right, moves independently in one of the most disquieting moments in Schumann's oeuvre. The skipping accompanies the first contrasting passage, a rich but somber tune in the left hand, with the second a thunderous and passionate chord sequence set in a slightly different skipping rhythm. In a hair-raising stroke of genius Schumann ends *Kreisleriana* with the skipping dropping away, quiet but menacing, at the bottom of the keyboard. Never overstated, shrewdly proportioned, at once witty and alarming, this passage shows the composer at the top of his game.

Fantasie, Op. 17

Schumann wrote this three-movement work partly to raise funds for a monument to Beethoven in Bonn, that composer's hometown. Sonata-like but unorthodox, the *Fantasie* contains one musical quotation from the last song in *An die ferne Geliebte*—"To the Distant Beloved"—Op. 98—Beethoven's song-cycle of 1816. (Schumann's reference provides a good excuse to get to know to *An die ferne Geliebte*, in case you haven't heard it.) There's also a passage in the last movement with a resemblance to Beethoven's work that's not as obvious a reference.

The *Fantasie* is probably Schumann's boldest take on the classical instrumental sonata. It's also quite possibly his supreme accomplishment, a composition in which beauty, passion, and mastery of form stand, for once, on equal footing. If you've never heard the work, the passion and beauty will be obvious; less clear is the composer's achievement in overall structure and in bending the sonata to his own ends, particularly in the first movement. Schumann's overall conception is bold, as well. A typical three-movement sonata of the classical era by Mozart or Beethoven will have fast outer movements surrounding a slow second movement. Here Schumann places his slow finale after two fast movements. A more conventional imagination would put the second movement's march of triumph last; but the slow finale, like that of Beethoven's last piano sonata (his Op. 111, and in two movements, by the way), offers solace of a different order.

What makes the first movement so remarkable is how Schumann stretches the form, adding a large, very unclassical digression; also staying true to his style by working with fragmentary ideas. These he does while keeping the whole in order, moving forward, and never redundant. Another more esoteric factor in his success relates to how he manages tonality, meaning the key. Nominally it's C major, but actually only on the last page does the composer steer the music there.[7]

Schumann's ability to transform a musical convention into something with new urgency and meaning comes right at the beginning, with the rolling figuration that accompanies the passionate opening theme. First, it's unusual for the left-hand accompaniment to precede the theme onstage; and then, this is no standard broken chord but instead the opening theme itself, compressed and speeded up. The main theme itself, crashing in notes and chords, is filled with passion, wonder, despair, and other nameless affects. (Schumann seems to have drafted the first movement, which is notable for its outbursts of pain, when he believed Clara Wieck to be lost to him.) Its phrasing is admirably flexible, refusing to settle into one of the composer's typical ruts. A second iteration is decorated with trills and a fiery change of key. But soon the flow is lost in fragmented reflections, ideas that shift, and halting changes of speed. A majestic tolling idea appears in the left hand, reawakening the opening theme which is restated climactically amid wild trills. These quiet down, leading to a new episode, slower and solemn, marked to be played "in the tone of a legend." This impressive idea is squarish, surely in deliberate contrast to what surrounds it. The legend is subjected to leisurely and beautiful exploration. No typical classical era sonata movement stops two-thirds of the way through for a new idea like this.

The initial idea returns, abruptly, in C minor, trailed by its subsidiary ideas that include the fragmented sequence. Finally, Schumann finds home tonally as the passionate opening theme (finally in C major) gives way to the heart-easing phrase from *An die ferne Geliebte*, elemental in its rise and fall, played four times, each more slowly and tenderly.

Set in three sections with a big coda, the second movement is a triumphal march. The rolled chords that open it are impressive, and the ideas that follow well varied, with rhythmic, dynamic (volume) and textural alterations that stave off monotony. Contrasts of phrasing and rhythmic shifts keep the profusion of ideas in the slower, charmingly strange middle section fresh and interesting. Some, for example, rush ahead impetuously while others pull back. The reiteration of the march is more emphatic than the first statement. The coda, seemingly described by every commentator as "notorious," consists of big jumps at high speed to the ends of the keyboard and back to the center. In live performance few pianists get through it without mistakes, sometimes by the handful, but even so the passage makes a thrilling end to the movement.

A blending of nocturne and hymn, the finale, like the two preceding movements, consists of remarkably diverse material. Following some arpeggios, a ruminative idea enters in the bass, followed by a melody buried in far-flung figuration that resembles a passage from the second movement of Beethoven's Piano Concerto No. 5 ("Emperor"). A solemn, prayerful idea deep in the bass leads to the movement's most important theme: a speechlike idea (long-long-short-long-long) that leads gradually but steadily to an ecstatic and thunderous climax. The second half basically repeats the material, ending the work as published on the arpeggios that opened it, here rising in excitement, then quieting, and a few soft chords.

As is often the case with Schumann, there's also an alternate ending of the third movement, recalling that of the first movement, with the Beethoven quotation. Found in a Budapest library, the alternate represents the composer's original conception.[8] Its cyclical effect is more powerful than the arpeggios and chords, broadening the structure of the entire *Fantasie*. Charles Rosen described, performed, and pushed for this ending, but it hasn't caught on yet. Rosen can be heard playing it on the compact disc accompanying *The Romantic Generation*; there are a couple of performances on YouTube, as well. It's well worth seeking out.

Arabeske, Op. 18
Blumenstück, Op. 19

Two lighter works, both easy to grasp and to like. The *Arabeske* is more frequently played and consequently more familiar. It's in a form known as a rondo, where a main section is interspersed with episodes of contrasting character. The opening section is a gentle melodic sequence set in dusty harmonies. The first episode has a plaintive character, and is trailed by a beautiful reflective passage that must have started as an improvisation. Set in a striding rhythm, the second episode feels more purposeful. Schumann ends the work with another reflective quasi-improvisation. The *Blumenstück*—"Flower-Piece"—is a set of five variations on a delicate theme. Rediscovered periodically by pianists, the *Blumenstück* is pleasant and pretty, an island of calm among its more turbulent kin.

Humoreske, Op. 20

Most listeners and musicians would agree that Schumann's fertility and daring in the *Humoreske* are still high. But the work is also a mess, exposing the composer's weaknesses as an editor and self-critic. Its closest relative is probably *Kreisleriana*, but it lacks the unity of tone and purpose that turn that work's contrasts into an aesthetic whole. Whereas *Kreisleriana* is dark, this is relatively cheerful and even giddy in spots. Here Schumann stays mostly in two closely related keys, but this tactic isn't enough to hold everything together. The *Humoreske*'s three lyrical interludes all seem reminiscent of the second part of *Kreisleriana*, with the third and last of them a step down in quality from the others and too long, as well. There are plenty of other moments that evoke *Kreisleriana* and more than a few echoes of the *Fantasiestücke*, as well, giving a slightly warmed-over feeling to the whole. That said, there are many moments in the *Humoreske* to enjoy, particularly in the opening section, and two of the three lyrical parts are meditations on long-limbed melodies that one can only admire.

Set in an unusual five-part structure, the opening section starts with a lovely Eusebian melody—somewhat reminiscent of *Des Abends* from *Fantasiestücke*—that hovers over a falling broken chord figure. Following a pause, the next passage contrasts completely with the opening in character. It's a bouncy but delicate tune of great appeal, which moves into a figure that's even more dashing and energetic, then to a more repetitious passage featuring triplets over a bouncing figure in the left hand. The tune of delicate bounce makes a welcome return, with the section ending on an abbreviated version of the hovering melody. Similar in its delicate mood, the second section features a tender, hesitant melody in the left hand beneath shuddering figuration in the right, but there's also a third line in the score. Marked "inner voice," it's a very Schumannesque concept, a melody that's implied but not actually played. This is followed by more quick, agitated ideas, and a section that resembles in a clog dance in chunky chords that's not unlike several of the *Fantasiestücke*.

Now the weaknesses and derivative aspect of the *Humoreske* start to poke through, as the third of its big sections essentially recapitulates the second part of *Kreisleriana*. There's another spacious and symmetrical melody explored at great length, with a central section consisting of busy passagework that's unmistakably similar to the first interlude in *Kreisleriana*'s second movement. The fourth section opens with another leisurely and beautiful tune, followed by another more sharply profiled idea alongside boiling figuration that seems to have a number of antecedents in *Kreisleriana*. This one moves into a continuous acceleration, leading to a thunderous figure in a sharp rhythm the composer indicates is to be played "with a bit of pomp." It's a great, rather funny idea; but it's hard not to wonder what it's doing here, as it seems isolated from what came before, what follows, and everything else in the *Humoreske*. Perhaps Schumann felt it too good to waste. A half-pause leads into the closing part, yet another slow melodic sequence that must have developed in the composer's improvisations. Inferior to the first two lyrical interludes, this one also meanders at length before Schumann ends the *Humoreske* with a brisk closing phrase.

Noveletten, Op. 21

Schumann described these as "extended, interconnected adventure stories";[9] the meaning of the title, "Novelettes," begins to make sense as one gets to know these bold and underappreciated works, several of which have clear narrative or pictorial qualities. It would be interesting to know whether and how well later composers, such as Mussorgsky, Wagner, Debussy, Ravel, and Stravinsky, knew them, as they do seem to anticipate achievements in tone painting by those masters.

The shortest of the *Noveletten* has a three-minute playing time, whereas the longest—the last of the eight—takes between ten and twelve minutes. These are big-boned works, larger in scope than their ancestors, the *Fantasiestücke*. Densely textured and hard to play, these show a return to the composer's concern with virtuosity, without however neglecting content, which is admirable and well organized, too. The roots of Brahms's late solo piano works can be found here. For some reason, *Noveletten* is rarely performed complete.

The first and most popular of the set opens with one of the composer's trademarked chunky chord sequences in an easy-gaited march. The contrasting passage that follows is a more tender Eusebian reply that also happens to be foursquare. This relatively straightforward piece alternates several flowing ideas with the opening chords. The second *Novelette* is a fierce technical study featuring a tiring spinning figure for the right hand over slashing chords in the left. It's interrupted by a spacious, proto-Brahmsian interlude in which lyrical phrases that aren't fully formed melodies flow easily out of triplet figuration. The spinning figure and chords return to round things out in a stormy yet triumphant conclusion reminiscent of the studies of Chopin and of Paganini.

The third *Novelette* presents a series of rhythmic puzzles and other technical challenges. The opening section is skittish and playful, with frequent changes in emphasis. The long middle part looks back at moods and keyboard figuration heard in the *Davidsbündlertänze*. Here the player has to juggle rapid chords and passionate outbursts in a darker affect. Schumann returns to the opening ideas to end the work on a lighter note. The fourth *Novelette* is a fast-moving dance suite in five well differentiated sections reminiscent of Weber's *Invitation*, some waltzes of Chopin's, and *Papillons*. A mood of irony is set by the disruptive accents and playful rhythms that saturate the opening waltz. The eloquent passage that follows has the immediacy of speech. The third section is a return of the opening, followed by a continually accelerating figuration, then ending with a last look at the opening waltz idea. Here there's a clear sense that a story set in a ballroom is being told from shifting, proto-cinematic points of view.

Narrative and pictorial elements can be found in the fifth *Novelette*, where musical impressions of a crowded scene, perhaps at a fair or festival, may be heard if one listens imaginatively. This is a long, multipart work, with a bustling momentum and jostling of its cheerful material. If you're familiar with Chopin's polonaises, this is dominated by the same rhythmic figure that energizes those great works. The jovial busyness of the opening page, the mood enhanced by much staccato writing, sets the scene. A quieter, contrasting section in a more flowing rhythmic incarnation follows, perhaps suggesting a quiet spot in the shade. After a return of the opening idea, a more tender duetlike idea in a short phrase over a pulsing accompaniment suggests another change of mood, probably an amorous exchange. The opening idea returns once more, to be interrupted by a fanfarelike passage suggesting a passing distraction. The composer revisits the opening, then the flowing idea, ending the piece quietly on the bouncing opening rhythm set against the more tender, duetlike phrase. The progress of any number of important musical depictions of a crowd at a festival, including those in Wagner's *Die Meistersinger von Nürnberg*, Debussy's *Fêtes*, and Stravinsky's *Petrushka*, may well originate in this *Novelette*. It's important, beautiful, and deserves to be better known.

Prefiguring Brahms in its breadth and richness, the sixth *Novelette* is easy to like. Although it opens with a scampering theme similar to that of the third of the series, the composer spins his ideas out here with a relaxed poise. The alternating playful and lyrical ideas flow so quickly and smoothly that there's never a sense of incongruity. The closing passage is fascinating, too, for its open-endedness. Brahms is also anticipated in the more tightly structured seventh of the series, which opens with a symmetrical melodic phrase that flies rapidly up and down the keyboard. The lyrical middle section presents a long, lilting melody over sweeping broken chords, reminiscent of passages in earlier works of Schumann's, perhaps most obviously the *Davidsbündlertänze*.

The last *Novelette* is also the one with the most vivid narrative structure, but as this is abstract music we can only guess at what it relates. The work opens with a surging and passionate melody over a boiling accompaniment similar in its troubled mood and keyboard layout to the start of *Kreisleriana*. A well-defined pause leads to the next idea, set in a prancing rhythm that differs radically from the opening in profile and affect, suggesting a new, more innocent character, a change of scene, or both. The opening theme slips back in, at first in hints, then in its full breadth. Now another new, jolly-sounding idea set in the same rhythm as the finale of the *Études symphoniques* enters. What has to be understood about this phrase is that it's a musical portrayal of joviality, much like a fictional description or as depicted a painting. Set at an ironic distance, it's a display of Schumann's narrative technique. In an unusual procedure, the composer introduces a long-drawn melodic phrase, describing it in the score as "A voice in the distance";[10] that and the obsessive rhythm, which continues on its way, seem to move along completely separate paths. The two alternate in their quiet noncompetition, ending the first part of the work. Apparently more cheerful, the second part opens with one of the composer's trademark clog dances, but this one is interrupted regularly by disturbances, some in the form of eerie harmonic shifts; another in a passionate outburst that moves to a majestic reincarnation of the "voice in the distance," the affective high point not only of this piece but of the entire set. Troubled to the last, the clog dance ends the work in an ambiguous tone. Throughout this remarkable work, the sense of characters in a powerful narrative is impossible to escape.

Sonata No. 3 in G Minor, Op. 22

Without question the most tightly constructed of the three sonatas, the Third is solid and well proportioned. Its chief problem is that the first and last movements are unrelievedly foursquare in their phrasing. Also, at Clara's request, Schumann unwisely abandoned an earlier version of the finale that's better than its replacement.

Unrelieved anxiety is the chief affect of the opening movement, where the first thematic group including the surging opening phrase and an idea in a stabbing rhythm add to its relentless sense of stress. Even the lyrical second theme might display more mellowness but for the pulsing of nervous sixteenth notes in the background. A big problem throughout is that the phrasing is stuck in a four-bar pattern; on the plus side, there's no fat and Schumann whips it all along at a fierce clip.

The two central movements also display admirable concision, and even compression in the case of the third-movement scherzo. The slow second movement sets songlike melodic phrases over accompaniments that pulse and flow along easily. This one of the composer's most successful adaptations of a classical era slow movement. Mozart set hundreds of elegant, aria-like tunes above flowing accompaniments in his instrumental works; Schumann's sounds instead like a German lied. With a playing time of under two minutes, the scherzo is a taut series of playful, slightly menacing ideas placed into in a sequence of tense rhythmic games.

As noted, there are two versions of the finale. The earlier, known by its tempo indication as the *Presto passionato*, was dropped at Clara's request. She thought it too challenging for the public and for other pianists. Schumann should have ignored her advice, as the *Presto passionato* is superior in every way to its replacement. Technically challenging but passionate and beautiful, the ideas are set forth with great sweep and a rhythmic complexity that the second finale lacks. The rondo that takes its place is put together with decent material but is burdened with square phrasing that's even more regular than that of the first movement. If you want to hear both versions in sequence, they have been recorded in a fine and revealing performance by Canadian pianist Anton Kuerti. Others have also recorded the *Presto passionato*.

Nachtstücke, Op.23

Four character pieces written in the depression Schumann experienced following the death of his brother, the "Night-Pieces" suffer from a lack of focus. The march rhythm of the first allows the composer to fall all too easily into a four-bar rut. Longest in the set, the second seems like an improvisation written down without editing or tightening. The chords of its opening phrase are a tired rehash of the sixteenth section of the *Davidsbündlertänze*. Best of the *Nachtstücke* is the third, a sweeping waltz. The composer makes a striking contrast to the waltz with a passage of scampering chords at a faster tempo. Last is another quasi-improvisational piece featuring a saccharine melody, wearily predictable in its four-bar phrasing, carried by arpeggios in the left hand.

Faschingsschwank aus Wien, Op. 26

The intimidating German title translates unpromisingly as "Carnival Jest from Vienna." It also carries the subtitle *Fantasiebilder*—"Fantastic Pictures"—which does nothing to dispel a sense of déjà vu: what new ground could the composer possibly be covering here? The answer is little, but this work is trim and well put together, if less ambitious and much along the same lines than any number of previous pieces. The title refers to the Lenten carnivals in Vienna, where Schumann composed it in 1838. No one claims it's his greatest work, but it's more than a few of steps up from the *Nachtstücke*, and better organized than *Humoreske*, if not as inspired as that uneven creation in its best moments. *Faschingsschwank* sounds fresher and more appealing when listened to either on its own or before other of the early piano works, where its similarity to prior compositions is less obtrusive.

Schumann blends elements of the character suite with sonata forms in *Faschingsschwank*. There are five sections, the first a big rondo with a vigorous, chordal main theme alternated with five episodes of contrasting character, several also of high energy. Reminiscent in mood of the suites of character pieces, all the elements are dancelike, with the lyrical first and swaying third episodes perhaps most readily enjoyable. But the entire movement is of good material well put together, as the composer finds a more traditional way of assembling his ideas. Titled *Romanze*, the second movement is a short, free meditation on a falling melody that's liedlike in character. Schumann lets the grave beauty of the tune speak for itself without overstatement. Third comes a *Scherzino*—"Little Scherzo"—on a catchy dance theme that seems to have been waiting for someone to write it. This is the likeliest moment of the work to stick with you initially.

The beautiful *Intermezzo* that follows is yet another reincarnation of the *Kreisleriana* opening, with a passionate minor-key theme riding on waves of urgent triplets. You may recall that the final *Novelette* opens with a similar idea, as does the second *Romanze* of *Drei Romanzen*, Op. 28. Schumann was haunted by this thematic profile, and lucky that he could find different ways to say it, all worth hearing. The solemn closing phrase, with its shift to the major, clearly inspired Brahms, who ends several of his late keyboard works in similar fashion. Perhaps the composer's most successful structure in a classical style so far, the brilliant finale sounds as though it could have been written by Beethoven. Here, Schumann uses contrasting material, all more neutral than usual, putting his themes effectively through the busy twists and turns of sonata form. The lyrical second theme, for instance, is unusually elegant for a composer who tends to favor thick keyboard textures.

Drei Romanzen, Op. 28

The second "Romance" is much played and popular, but the first is also good. The third is the longest and weakest. The first opens with the now familiar *Kreisleriana* pattern of a surging, passionate melody crashing over a boiling triplet accompaniment. Beautiful like its relatives, this one is reinforced by booming bass notes and a rich-sounding dissonance. The second "Romance" is the most familiar of the three, consisting of a tranquil slow melody that turns gently between accompaniment in both hands. Like its sibling, the second movement of *Faschingsschwank aus Wien*, the theme is displayed in all its beauty without overstatement. Third and least is a piece based on a marchlike idea interspersed with two contrasting interludes, both of which are better than the main theme. The first interlude is fleet and graceful, the second lush; unfortunately, the primary idea surrounding them is annoyingly spiky and thin, and Schumann repeats it too many times.

Scherzo, Gigue, Romanze und Fughette, Op. 32

Schumann's early keyboard period ends with four little sketches, not terribly significant but unpretentious. The scherzo is a playful exercise set mostly in a skipping rhythm. Accelerations, slowdowns, stops, and starts contribute to its skittish mood. The gigue is a lilting dance form from the baroque era. Schumann's well-made little specimen is saturated in counterpoint. In the *Romanze*, he sets one of his trademarked passionate ideas over a chattering accompaniment, with a contrasting middle section. The phrasing is predictable and square. Actually another gigue, the *Fughette* is probably the most interesting of the four. As the title ("Little Fugue") suggests, the textures are contrapuntal, but its pungent harmonies are intriguing, and the work has an irresistible charm.

Schumann's production for solo piano thins out considerably after 1840. Most important by a long way are the *Waldszenen*—"Forest Scenes"—Op. 82, completed in 1849. There are occasionally others, but there's no question that the composer's attention and interest had turned in other directions.

Album für die Jugend, Op. 68

The "Album for the Young" is an extensive (43-part) collection of mostly easier works, as the title implies. Unlike the *Kinderszenen*, these really are intended for children and beginners at the piano. If you've studied the piano or lived close to a student, you've probably heard one or more of them. Many are very straightforward, consisting of nothing more than a single melodic line in the right hand against the simplest of accompaniments in the left, with one note per hand. Others are chord progressions of the plainest sort. Some, such as the *Volkslied*—"Folksong"—(number 9) and *Errinerung*—"Memory"—feature warm melodies that have become familiar as cultural background. The broken chord study that is number 14 is both simple and beautiful, as is the tender sketch called *Mignon* (number 36). But quite a few are bigger in scope and far from easy. Perhaps the best known of the more demanding studies is the twelfth, *Knecht Ruprecht*—"Knight Rupert"—a fierce character portrait. Closest to the Schumann of the poetic early works are the untitled numbers 21 and 30, warm-hearted and reflective melodies with more complex accompaniments than most in the series. An excellent example of tone-painting can be heard in number 39, the second of two with the title *Winterszeit*—"Wintertime." The chiming and skipping of number 40 represent a paired prelude and fugue in the manner of J. S. Bach. These are not difficult to listen to, but you have to keep in mind that Schumann's purpose is fundamentally didactic.

Like many musicians, Schumann found counterpoint in the hands of Bach overwhelming. The older master regularly stirred and struck terror into legions of followers for the ease and expressive force of his techniques, and Schumann was no exception. Like Mozart and Chopin (who closed letters to his students with the salutation "practice Bach"[11]), Schumann made several studies of counterpoint, with the predictable result that he produced work that's more contrapuntally inflected. As is common among later composers, the knowledge gained results in enriched musical textures. Of the works from these middle years, the *Vier Fugen*—"Four Fugues"—Op. 72, are perhaps the most attractive. This is so largely because Schumann wrote them more in his own style rather than imitating Bach, which he also did with less success. These four short works, with their dusky tonal coloring, represent an approach to the style that effectively fuses his high-romantic manner to the old technique.[12]

Waldszenen, Op. 82

"Forest Scenes," a set of nine more or less independent character pieces is well known and popular. Typically for Schumann, they're inconsistent. Several of them are very good, a couple perhaps less so, and one, *Vogel als Prophet*, utterly great. While there's much to like, "[*Waldszenen*] also betrays how true it is that much of the earlier energy had abandoned his genius. . . ."[13]

Eintritt—"Entry"—is a dull-sounding title for the beauties of this opening section, in which a tender melody emerges from a gently pulsing accompaniment into which a figure that suggests a rustic horn call[14] is built. A proto-impressionistic haze seems to cover the piece, as the composer also displays unusually flexibility in his phrasing. The sharp springing rhythms and fiery passagework of *Jäger auf der Lauer*—"Hunter in Ambush"—contrast absolutely with *Eintritt*. It's a good if somewhat obvious example of tone-painting. With its very regular, sugary melody, *Einsame Blumen*—"Solitary Flowers"—is a more ordinary conception of a profile we've heard before from the composer. He does however work in some attractive harmonic effects toward the end.

Schumann employs patterns of the French overture, a baroque form, in *Verrufene Stelle*—"Haunted Spot." In this, one of the better elements of the set, the composer wittily adapts the patterns of the old style to achieve a spooky mood, though nothing of a *Kreisleriana*-like menace is remotely suggested here. His textural methods include the alternation of phrases with a sharp rhythmic profile with others in a stalking mode, laid out in steady staccato notes. The pretty *Freundliche Landschaft*—"Friendly Landscape" sets a relaxed mood with easily rolling triplets. Also comfortable in a very nineteenth-century German way is *Herberge*—"At the Inn." The material is similar to that of the opening movement, but here the easygoing mood seems forced, and *Herberge* also lacks the beauties and the breadth of *Eintritt*.

Wonderfully strange, *Vogel als Prophet* stands as the high point of the *Waldszenen*, and a landmark in the composer's later career. The title, which is usually translated as "The Prophet-Bird," is puzzling, but you'll get the point when you hear this magical piece where Schumann uses the keyboard to imitate birdcalls that seem to speak in prophetic tones. The birdcall is rendered initially in a five-note phrase (*long*-short-short-short-*long*) that moves with great deliberation up and down the keyboard, hovering generally but not exclusively in the upper registers. Sometimes it's varied with a descending figure in a steadier bouncing rhythm. The accompaniment consists of mostly simple notes and chords that support the more elaborate melodic material. A contrasting central passage is unusually brief, consisting of chords in the tonic major key, but its haunted mood never breaks the eerie atmosphere. The work ends on a complete restatement of the opening idea.

The idea that a bird is singing not just comprehensibly but prophetically reminds us poignantly of the composer's fragile sanity; yet it's here that Schumann recaptures the glorious strangeness of his early period. In its delicacy *Vogel als Prophet* even has a leg up on much of his early work. It seems likely that the notably sane Maurice Ravel took a cue from Schumann in *Oiseaux tristes*—"Sad Birds," second of the *Miroirs*, his great suite of tone paintings for the keyboard. Ravel opens his work with a solemn bird call similar to Schumann's, and the entire piece is also densely saturated with impressions of birdcalls.

There's nothing delicate about *Jagdlied*—"Hunting Song," the hearty and difficult chord study that follows. Set in three parts, the quieter central section offers a welcome contrast with its skittish rhythmic profile and lower dynamics. Longest in the set, *Abschied*—"Farewell," is an extended and tranquil reflection in long melodic lines set over pulsing chords at the center of the keyboard. There's an autumnal feel to this, the beautiful and expansive conclusion to the *Waldszenen*.

A few remaining works merit mention, if not detailed examination. The *Bunte Blätter*—"Pretty Leaves"—Op. 99, are an assortment of fourteen works from the 1830s that the composer assembled for publication in 1850. There are promising titles for the individual pieces (there's a *Novelette*, for instance) but these are in fact a random assortment, some fragmentary and others in desperate need of editing. There are works of quality among them: Brahms used one as the subject of his Variations on a Theme by Schumann, Op. 9. The twenty *Albumblätter*—"Album Leaves"—Op. 124, have the same origin and can be viewed the same way, with minor finds among them if you take the trouble to listen. Attempts are regularly made to reintroduce the six-part *Gesänge der Frühe*—"Songs of the Dawn"—Op. 133, of 1853. But despite moments of beauty they are hopelessly static, and quite unlike the earlier Schumann. In the third, just as in the finale of the *Études symphoniques*, the composer settles into a rhythmic figure that he can't get out of. Perhaps the best is the stormy fourth, which at least echoes Schumann at his finest and must have inspired Brahms, whose great character works for solo piano works follow similar patterns. The familiar and promising title of the three *Fantasiestücke*—"Fantasy Pieces"—Op. 111, of 1851 similarly offer no surprises with their three-part formats but are concise and well made. The first piece is one last *Kreisleriana*-esque surging melody over a boiling accompaniment; the second a tender melodic sequence with a contrasting central section; the third, a quirky march. Overall, Schumann's Op. 111 is probably the most consistent and satisfying of his late works for solo keyboard.

4 The Concertos and Other Works for Solo Instruments and Orchestra

The Piano Concerto, Op. 54, is for good reason the most played and familiar in this category; nearly two hundred recordings of the work are currently on the market. Schumann also composed a late, dreary concerto for cello that's reasonably familiar, and an equally unmemorable violin concerto from 1853 that's infrequently performed. The four shorter pieces include a couple of lesser items for piano and violin and a concerto-like work for four horns and orchestra. But the big game here is indeed the Piano Concerto, lyrical, well made, and easy to like.

Piano Concerto in A Minor, Op. 54

Schumann first conceived this work in 1841 as a single-movement "Fantasy for Piano and Orchestra." In only slightly altered form this would later serve as the finished concerto's first movement. He completed the piece four years later, adding a slow movement and a finale, bringing the work up to the standard form of a classical-era concerto. The first movement displays his comfort with sonata form, which he finally handles with ease; similarly, the orchestration breaks no ground but is more than serviceable. The beauty of the thematic material and the tight, nearly continuous dialogue between the keyboard and accompaniment are what give the work its appeal. Vigorous, masculine, charming, and soulful, the concerto is no sense a virtuoso vehicle, but rather a lyrical masterwork that puts some of the composer's best qualities on display.

Schumann's tempo and expression marking for the first movement is unusual and worth noting: "*Allegro affetuoso*"—"quick and with tenderness." The opening phrase consists of cascading proclamatory chords that clearly influenced Norwegian composer Edvard Grieg in writing the opening of his single, equally well-loved piano concerto, also in the same key. Although Schumann's opening phrase seems rhetorical, it's in fact thematic, as it is integrated into the structure of the movement. The multifaceted main theme has a big personality, in part reflective, warmhearted, and a bit melancholy. It's set first on chords for the woodwinds, echoed by the soloist, immediately following the dramatic opening flourish. The sweeping phrase that follows displays animation, energy, as well as an autumnal richness, although the composer was only thirty-one when he conceived it. A variety of ideas mostly lyrical, some more lively are built into a forceful climax. This gives way to the development, here a long section beginning with a dreamlike dialogue between the soloist and the clarinet, at a slower tempo and in a distant tonality. A typical classical-era development typically subjects themes to all kinds of fantastical disruptions. But Schumann seems to like his beautiful ideas too much to break them up as Haydn, Mozart, or Beethoven might. Here, the material is treated tenderly and with little sense of sonata form conflict. The dramatic opening flourish is brought back and given its own reexamination, followed by an urgent reiteration of the main theme, shared by the soloist and the winds, led by the flute. Satisfying the classical structure, this passage returns to the opening sequence, which is repeated, here without the cascading chords. Schumann also follows traditions with a cadenza, a virtuosic passage for the soloist, this one meditative and lyrical in his best manner. As is normal, the cadenza leads into the final section (the coda), and an exciting quick-time passage where the main theme is transformed into a headlong march rhythm.

Described by the composer as an "intermezzo," the relatively brief slow movement moves in ways that contrast with the sweeping flows of the concerto's outer sections. Instead of the long-limbed ideas impelling those, this opens with a relaxed phrase that chugs along gently, with sighing commentary from the woodwinds. By way of contrast, Schumann introduces an overripe melody for the cellos, joined by the woodwinds, which the keyboard decorates. The chugging theme returns for another iteration. But a slight slowing of the tempo and a shift to a remote key bring an echo of the opening movement from the winds and a descending reply, dreamily reminiscent of the chordal sequence that opened the concerto, leading without pause to the finale.

Like the first movement, the third is cast in sonata form. The opening theme is a virile, energetic idea with a yodeling quality, set to a waltzlike beat. Its profile also resembles the first movement's, although not literally. In any case, it's vividly memorable and is likely to stick with you on first hearing. The more lyrical second theme is set out first in delicate passagework, then a more richly autumnal incarnation that also echoes the first movement. Apart from a mock-stormy phrase or passage here and there the affects the composer summons are never anything other than cheerful and even joyous. Perhaps Schumann's only lapse is in the development where the strings take a weak stab at a fugal passage. It's brief, however, and the delicate and burlier incarnations of the main themes are skillfully interwoven right to the end.

Introduction and Allegro appassionato, Op. 92
Introduction and Allegro, Op. 134

Both are substantial, technically well-made, fifteen-minute works for piano and orchestra. Schumann composed Op. 92 in 1849, Op. 134 in 1853. If you listen to them after the Piano Concerto, you'll hear a diminution of that work's big, appealing personality that's pronounced in the case of Op. 92 and genuinely startling in Op. 134. The interwoven arpeggios for the keyboard with the horn, clarinets, and strings of the Introduction and Allegro appassionato are lovely. Once the main section marked by barking brass begins, however, the work seems to turn into a sequence of predictable postclassical gestures, right down to the empty triumph of the ending. The loss of genuine feeling with the gestural taking its place is complete in Op. 134. Perhaps the best that can be said is that it sounds rather like the music of the young Brahms (to whom it was dedicated), especially one pleasant, winding melodic phrase for the woodwinds.

Concert-piece (*Konzertstück*) in F Major for four horns, Op. 86

Cello Concerto in A Minor, Op. 120

Violin Concerto in D Minor, without opus number (composed in 1853)

Phantasie for Violin and Orchestra in C Major, Op. 131

With the exception of the work for four horns, listening to Schumann's late-period works for solo instruments and orchestra is a depressing experience. Despite being carefully assembled, all of these betray an emptiness, a lack of passion and purpose, that's impossible to deny. None of them (again, except for Op. 86) is made of thematic material that's even remotely memorable, and certainly not like Schumann's early period. The composer dutifully obeys classical forms, but he's spinning notes rather than speaking from the heart. It's hard to believe that they're written by the same wild soul and encoder of secret musical messages who conceived the great early works. Advocates claim to find in them greater delicacy and more finished compositional techniques, and they do seem, again, to have been useful to Brahms. The younger composer's two concertos for strings (for violin, Op. 77, and the Double Concerto for Violin and Cello, Op. 102) pick up on hints from Schumann that the younger master was able to develop and magnify, especially in the finales, which in both of the Brahms works are interesting, beautiful, and thrilling.

Composed in 1849, the *Konzertstück* for horns is fully worked out three-movement concerto. No one claims it's Schumann's greatest work, but Op. 86 displays the freedom, energy, and playfulness uniformly lacking in the later works for strings. The only catch is that the brassy sound of the four soloists may be over the top for some listeners.

5 The Chamber Music

Except for state executions and music, the word chamber has little use these days. And there's probably no term that has discouraged more potential listeners from enjoyment than this, reeking of all that's dull and elitist. Brevity seems to be the phrase's only quality. Several centuries old, *chamber music* refers to the secular setting, the room or chamber—*camera* in Italian—where it was performed, as opposed to a church, as interludes to services. (The latter works are called *sonatas da Chiesa*, with the last word meaning "church.") As time passed, its essence shifted to music for small ensembles of from two to nine or ten instruments, above which the group is considered a chamber orchestra.

Chamber music is certainly a serious and noble category, though, with composers from Haydn on often reserving ideas, experiments, and processes that are better worked through with forces smaller than a symphony orchestra. Chamber ensembles offer composers better forums for intimate discussion between a few instruments. Another reason for its appeal to the eighteenth-century masters who transformed the genre was that chamber music was generally performed at home, by amateur players. Sonata forms dominate chamber music, with the majority of chamber works nothing more than sonatas for instrumental ensembles, similar in structure to those for solo piano.

The roll call of great classical-era chamber music is awe inspiring, from Haydn's string quartets and piano trios to Mozart's string quintets (along with countless other works by that master) and Beethoven's string quartets, which represent a high water mark intimidating to later composers. Beethoven's experiments in his string quartets ran ahead of his nineteenth-century followers including Schumann, whose efforts show Beethoven's influence but are more conservative.

Although he sketched material for chamber ensembles earlier, many of Schumann's chamber works were generated in a brief, intensely productive period in 1842. These include his most popular chamber work, the Quintet for Piano and Strings, Op. 44, a radiant composition that needs little analysis to enjoy and appreciate. Also from that year are the Quartet for Piano and Strings, Op. 47, which is also marvelous, and undeservedly in the shadow of its bigger and more outgoing sibling, the Quintet; and the three String Quartets, Op. 41, which fall a step below, well made though they are. Despite its out of sequence opus number, the *Fantasiestücke*, Op. 88, for piano trio also dates from 1842. Schumann also wrote three full-scale piano trios later in his career; the first, Op. 63, speaks with real passion, while the last two display the composer's tendencies toward formalism and density of texture with a diminished clarity of expression. The same has to be said for a couple of late sonatas for violin and piano. There are also several unassuming works for strings and woodwinds with piano from Schumann's later career that are lyrically satisfying.

In an early display of Schumann's growing musical conservatism, his most important chamber works are in sonata form. It's here that we see the beginnings of the formalism that will ultimately choke off expressivity in so many of his late works. But in the best of the chamber works, perhaps most obviously the Piano Quintet, Op. 44, the composer's innate lyricism and manic high spirits easily win the day.

Schumann's chamber music differs from his early piano works in its reflection of his growing concern with structure. He is working more carefully here, making sure to obey the demands of sonata forms. Haydn, Mozart, and Beethoven tend to use material that's generic or with a pithy, mottolike character for sonata development. As we've seen, Schumann's early masterworks for keyboard contain wild and fantastical themes set in short, contrasting bursts of energy and reflection. For many this style shows his genius in its highest and most characteristic manner. But as the composer himself understood, such ideas are poorly suited to classical structural processes. So, it's here, in the chamber works, that a shift to plainer, more regular thematic material can be heard. That's not to suggest the primary themes are colorless or unattractive: in the best of the chamber works Schumann's imagination still overflows. But the main ideas tend to be more straightforward, with the wilder stuff worked in secondarily.

Quintet in E-flat Major for Piano and String Quartet, Op. 44

This big-boned, lovable composition has for good reason always been one of the composer's most popular. It's wonderful to be carried on its irresistible sweep of ideas, alternately high spirited and lyrical, with a haunting slow movement that's one of Schumann's greatest inspirations. The quintet for piano and string quartet is a form this composer appears to have invented. It's a big ensemble that makes an impressive, quasi-orchestral sound, with the composer's unfussy treatment of the instruments adding to its appeal. Schumann's Piano Quintet has a few well known offspring, including a great, youthful work by Brahms, another immensely popular one by Dvořák, and a fierce and gloomy quintet by Shostakovich.

Schumann's Quintet opens in a grand rush of sound for the full ensemble. The great, striding main theme has an almost tidal force but is filled as well with unambiguous joy. The strings, led by the first violin, plays a gentler iteration of the opening idea. Set in a similar rhythm, the second theme, given to the cello and piano, forms a tender and gracious reply to the flooding force of the opening phrase. Schumann's skill at classical thematic manipulation was never better than in the development section of this movement. (It's here that thematic material is broken apart, redistributed, expanded, compressed, and otherwise reexamined.) The composer moves this bright and energetic material to darker tonal regions, also opening his melodic material out into busy figuration and rhythmic shifts. The third section (the recapitulation) basically repeats the opening sequence, which Schumann accelerates into a driving coda.

One of his finest conceptions, the second movement is headed *In Modo d'una Marcia*—"In the Manner of a March," Track 19 on the CD at the back of the book. The title is important because the composer draws with it a distinction between his music and an actual funeral march, which it clearly evokes. What the listener can infer is that there's a slight, ironic distance between an actual march and this music. There are many precedents before Schumann of highly wrought, rarefied funeral marches by Handel, Mozart, Beethoven, Chopin, and others, with Schumann's as fine as any. These spaces between art and life can be perceived most clearly in the three interludes that share the stage with the main march theme that opens and ends the movement. It's built of a quiet, fanfarelike phrase followed by the march, simple and somber, interspersed with the composer's masterstroke in the form of carefully calculated pauses that make the tune unforgettable.

The first interlude is a very beautiful, solemn phrase in long lines shared by the strings to a keyboard accompaniment in gently pulsing triplets. Suggesting deep breathing, it's one of Schumann's most sublime ideas. The march is repeated, followed by a second episode, in a sharply contrasting stormy and agitated moods and quicker tempo. The composer works the march theme into its thick textures. Without interruption the long-breathed tune is brought back and explored once more, now fully revealing its consolatory nature. The movement ends with a quiet reiteration of the march, the strings now plucked (pizzicato) to create a drier, spent sound. Schumann structures the closing as a long fade-down in volume while holding to the steady march tempo.

The scherzo is more or less classical in structure, with two trios (the name for the interludes of contrasting character and texture) instead of the usual one. It has a driving energy reminiscent of Beethoven,[1] with an opening theme built around a rising scale that's also Beethovenian in its force and simplicity. Long, lilting lines for the strings and a gentle triplet accompaniment for the piano in the first of the two short trios recalls the slow movement's great lyrical interlude without its emotional weight. After a reiteration of the thunderous opening idea, the second trio strikes a completely different tone. Playfully grotesque, it's filled with dialogues for the plucked strings and keyboard and wild, scurrying passages for the ensemble. After one more iteration of the main idea, his inventiveness overflowing, the composer adds a coda in an ever-tightening rhythmic pattern.

The big closing movement is in a modified sonata form. It opens with a busy, attractive theme with a dancelike character, very high classical in feel, reminiscent of Beethoven or Schubert. The second theme is a rising idea for the keyboard accompanied by sighs from the strings. In this section, a new, powerfully lyrical idea emerges in the violins, underpinned by a marchlike figure. A climactic passage that ends in set of big chords for the full ensemble leads into a fugue based on the broad melody that opened the quartet. Schumann gives this cyclical return a full contrapuntal treatment, blending it with the catchy dance theme. As is sometimes the case, there's a slightly contrived quality to the fugal passage. It's relatively brief, however, and perhaps the only moment in this immensely appealing work to seem even a bit flat.

Quartet in E-flat Major for Piano, Violin, Viola, and Cello, Op. 47

You'll note that Schumann's ensemble here has one less violin than the Quintet, creating slightly less sound than the rather massive volume sometimes generated by its companion. The mood of the Quartet is also a bit less exuberant than that of the overflowing Op. 44. In the Quartet, the composer generally keeps to a postclassical profile, with more neutral material and a clear four movement structure. It's a work of high quality, also, though, requiring a bit more time to appreciate than its sibling.

The piano quartet with this same makeup—there are others for piano and winds—appears to have been invented by Mozart, who wrote two magnificent specimens (G Minor, K. 478, and E-flat Major, K. 493). There are also significant works in this category by Mendelssohn, Brahms, Dvořák, and the underappreciated French composer Gabriel Fauré, among others.

The first movement opens with a short passage that's slow in tempo and lyrically meditative. The main body of the movement opens with a phrase that combines briskness with lyricism. The second theme, in a minor key and easy lilting rhythm, contrasts well with the opening sequence. Schumann works the ideas together with energy and skill.

The meditative opening material, which seemed introductory is unexpectedly brought back. Here it's used to introduce the long development section, dominated by a four-note figure and a tense mood. But just as it seems headed for a dramatic climax, the main theme is brought back triumphantly instead. The composer expands his material in the recapitulation, bringing the opening sequence back yet again before an excited closing passage.

Schumann evokes the music of his friend Mendelssohn in the scherzo, which consists of a fast-moving idea in a call and response pattern reminiscent of moments from that master's incidental music for *A Midsummer Night's Dream*. As in scherzo of the Piano Quintet, there are two trios. The first is a long, low-profile melodic phrase, which Schumann treats in canon, a type of tight counterpoint. After a reprise of the movement's opening theme, the second trio consists of long-held chords that contrast radically with the scurrying motion of the main idea. This satisfying take on Mendelssohn's fairy music ends on a witty, carefully calculated fade-down of the primary phrase.

The lyrical melody that opens the slow third movement has a slightly tired feel that makes it perhaps the weakest idea in the work. The composer weaves his instrumental lines with reasonable charm and skill, however. But the slower, hymnlike passage that stands at the center of this three-part movement is more than a step up from the opening. A deeply touching paragraph in chords for the piano and canonic writing for the strings, it shows the extent of Schumann's study of Beethoven, resembling one of that master's great, expansive slow movements. The third section repeats the tired opening, decorating it with sixteenth notes by the piano and violin. Knowing a good idea when he has come up with one, Schumann recalls the Beethoven-like phrase without repeating it in full just before the end.

The finale is a high-energy sonata form essay with a lot of counterpoint woven in. It opens with a brisk chords followed by a rattling idea in falling sixteenth-notes, that are treated in *fugato*—like a fugue but not fully worked through. The counterpoint is broken off abruptly for a wonderful, lilting melody for the cello, accompanied by the other strings and piano that contrasts beautifully with the ever-resurgent counterpoint. There's lots of contrasting material here from a sighing, falling chromatic one to a brisk idea in pecking, repeated notes. Schumann works his themes together as he drives toward a triumphant reiteration of the movement's opening sequence, then cuts loose with a yet more impressive and energetic *fugato* in busily running sixteenth-notes, all building to an ecstatic climax, marked by arpeggios for the violin and viola. The gorgeous cello theme also makes a final appearance. Schumann's application of polyphony works better here than in the finale of Op. 44.

Three String Quartets, Op. 41

The most important ensemble in chamber music is the string quartet. Haydn, who invented it, composed eighty-three, more than half of which form the bedrock of the repertory. The ten quartets of Mozart's maturity, Beethoven's sixteen, and four of Schubert's fifteen essays in the form join Haydn's as the core of the high classical peak for the genre. As noted, Beethoven's monumental quartets from his middle and late periods, some in five, six, and seven movements, and in his sublime late style, carried the string quartet to unimagined heights, daunting to many who followed. Certainly Mendelssohn, Brahms, and Dvořák looked to more traditional patterns when writing theirs. It took a couple of generations for composers to find ways through the Beethoven problem. But by the late nineteenth and early twentieth century, Debussy, Ravel, Fauré, the Czech composer Janáček, and the Second Viennese School—Schoenberg, Berg, and Webern—had composed great string quartets in new, distinctive idioms. And the six by Bartók proved once and for all that the string quartet still had a great deal new to say. Later in the twentieth century, Shostakovich's fifteen and American composer Elliot Carter's five thorny quartets are all played and admired.

In his three string quartets, Schumann's debt to others, and Beethoven above all, is clear. It's a matter of personal taste in how well one thinks he dealt with the challenge of writing in this form only fifteen years after Beethoven's death, but it seems safe to say that they don't show Schumann at his idiosyncratic or high-spirited best. But they have their moments. He was still only thirty-two when he composed them, so his youthful energy was still with him. But generally Schumann seems straitjacketed rather than comfortable here.

The first quartet, in A minor, takes up Beethoven's challenges most directly and, perhaps, with the least success. The first movement is a clear takeoff on Beethoven's Quartet No. 14, Op. 131, generally agreed to be his greatest. Beethoven opens his seven-movement work with an ethereal fugue followed by a delicate and lilting dance. Following Beethoven's sequence, Schumann opens his first movement with a fugal passage followed by a dancelike movement in the same rhythm as Beethoven's second movement. The young Schumann's fugue has none of Beethoven's spirituality; the choreography of the main section makes for pleasant listening, if not a strong comparison with its weightless model. The scherzo that follows is, like the parallel movement of Schumann's Piano Quartet, a tribute to Mendelssohn's elfin style. The slow movement reveals a debt to Schubert. It's a leisurely affair based on a broad melody stated by the first violin. Some dramatic gestures toward the middle suggest a crisis, but these have none of the shock that Schubert offers in the slow movements of his late Piano Sonata in A Major (D. 959) or the String Quintet in C Major (D. 956). Schumann's finale is mostly an exercise on a rattling theme that's treated in pedestrian counterpoint. There's an unexpected shift as the composer turns to the major key with a droning, ecstatic Beethoven-like phrase. This is followed by a long choralelike sequence in quiet chords for the ensemble, with those two phrases forming the best passage in the movement.

The Quartet No. 2, in F major, works better than the first. It opens with an easily flowing, memorable lyrical idea that seems to be enough for the composer to build a satisfying structure. There's not even a contrasting second theme, but only a single melodic stream. Schumann pits melodic fragments from this lovely flow against each other in the minor-key development section, after which the opening melody makes an abbreviated return. The composer works in a beautiful sequence of floating chords just before the end. A series of four variations on a theme, the second movement again recalls late Beethoven. Here the model is clearly the slow movement of Beethoven's Quartet No. 12, Op. 127.[2] Again, Schumann can't plumb the same depths as Beethoven, but this is well put together, if a bit long. The short scherzo, set in a rocking, 6/8 beat, again recalls Mendelssohn. The weird comedy of the Trio is pure Schumann, however. The finale is a rondo, a form in which episodes of varying moods and profiles alternate with a recurring main theme. Here the chief idea has rustic character, like a country dance. The mood remains relaxed and cheerful, with moments of mock agitation, but no real stress or conflict.

Also lyrical, the Quartet No. 3 in A Major opens with a brief, slow introduction. A sighing figure that dominates the entire movement is presented four times. At a slightly quicker speed the sighing figure kicks off the main section, but as in the F Major Quartet none of the material varies widely in mood. The development has little real conflict, as new sequences built of long-held chords float above. The coda opens with one of these sequences, ending humorously with the cello exhaling the opening sigh deep in its baritone register. The most original section of the quartet, the second movement is a delicately troubled scherzo built on a different, more agitated sighing figure set in a lilting rhythm. Schumann calls for many passages to be repeated, an instruction not always followed, resulting in performances that differ radically in length. The better path (taken for example by the Quatuor Hermès) is to skip the repeats, keeping the momentum and allowing the inherent strangeness of the material to come through. The last passage of this variation-like movement is a forceful waltzlike iteration of the theme followed by a melting coda in the major key. Cast in three broad sections, the slow third movement is more conventional, consisting of a self-consciously sublime lyrical outer passage with a self-consciously agitated central part. The finale is a witty rondo cast in a Schubertian country-dance mold. The main theme is set in a comically stiff rhythm, with which all the episodes contrast effectively.

Piano Trio in D Minor, Op. 63

Like the string quartet, the ensemble for piano, violin, and cello known as the piano trio has a large and impressive repertory. Like the string quartet, Haydn developed it; his forty-five favor the keyboard but are no less wonderful for that and infinitely rewarding to hear. With one exception, the Trio in E Major, K. 542, Mozart's are a step below the absurdly high level of that master's best chamber works. Beethoven's six, which go from his early maturity to the last, the "Archduke" Trio (nicknamed for the patron it's dedicated to) are majestically scaled and at the highest expressive plane; Schubert composed only two, but both are big and important works. There are other good, fine, and great examples from the nineteenth and twentieth centuries by Mendelssohn, Brahms, Dvořák, Tchaikovsky, Fauré, and Shostakovich. And in its own class is Ravel's wonderful Piano Trio.

So, here, as with the string quartet, Schumann had stiff competition in his own lifetime. Schumann wrote the first two of his three piano trios in 1847 and the third in 1851. Their popularity drops as they go, with the first universally considered the best of the three and the last the least liked and performed. One of the composer's best works for chamber ensemble, the Trio No. 1 in D Minor recaptures much of the early period's thematic richness. Each movement is strong and the four are well matched and proportioned; Schumann also unifies the movements with subtle thematic links.

"With energy and passion" is the composer's promising expression mark for the first movement. The opening theme is a rising idea for the strings over a just-below boiling accompaniment for the piano. It's yet another descendant of the raging *Kreisleriana* idea, which as we see still haunted Schumann nine years later. Here it's less furious, but longer, more lyrical, and very beautiful. The contrasting second theme is set in chords in a sharp rhythm; before the passionately surging idea that rounds out the exposition comes a tiny, spectral echo of the chords. The development pits these well differentiated ideas against each other in interesting and beautiful ways, showing Schumann's skill at thematic elaboration. The otherworldly passage for the strings alongside pulsing triplets for the piano marks the heart of the development section; it's also one of the most striking ideas in a work filled with them. A slow-down recalls the pulsing theme in a major key before a majestic shift back to the somber home tonality, in the impressive coda.

The middle movements are carefully paired and not overlong. Clearly derived from the second theme of the first movement, the three-part scherzo is based on a rough dance idea in which even notes and accented chords alternate in a conflict-laden mood. The central trio is made of rising and falling lines for the strings in canonic imitation. Its textures contrast with those of the outer sections, but the affect remains tense. The opening theme of the slow movement is a mournful but noble tune of a Beethoven-like profile, sung by the strings to a rich keyboard accompaniment. Schumann brings back throbbing triplets for the middle section, which is also at a quicker tempo. The melodic material here is a fragmented but passionate duet for the violin and cello, with the piano acting as accompanist. Later, the keyboard gets to sing out the melodies.

The finale, which follows without pause, is based on a transformation of the opening movement's dominating idea into a vigorous marchlike tune, filled with strange, droning accents but full of inner life. Other ideas have a more spectral quality that again recalls the first movement. The development gives alternating, fragmented expression to both the vigor and the inwardness, rather like early Schumann but here in sonata form. And the breathless coda is an ever-accelerating reminder of the composer's manic nature, making for a thrilling ending to one of his best works for chamber ensemble.

Neither the Second nor the Third Piano Trios holds up nearly as well. Although composed later in the same year (1847) as the D minor work, the Trio No. 2 in F Major, Op. 80, feels constricted and overwritten. Never an overly polished writer for chamber ensembles, here Schumann is particularly heavy-handed, with all three instruments frequently playing at the same time. Another major problem with Op. 80 is that there's too much contrapuntal writing weighing the music down. In the hands of Bach, polyphony can easily carry the expressive weight. Like many composers, Schumann does better when he finds subtle ways of adapting counterpoint as a textural enrichment. Schumann was clearly obsessed with counterpoint when he wrote this Trio, and the work's momentum and impact suffer as a result.

The first movement opens with an attractive and promising leaping figure, but a cheerful mood is never fully established. This is surely because the composer's treatment, which leans heavily on busy counterpoint, is unnecessarily complex. The slow second movement is, like the first, thick in texture from start to finish. Schumann copies the slow movement of the first trio by making the contrasting middle section in a quicker tempo. This also feels overmanaged, although the composer intriguingly suggests a waltz rhythm while staying in 4/4 time. Without question, the third movement's strange, limping waltz is the best part of the work. It's as haunting as Schumann intended, holding up well to repeated listening, surely also because he uses the ensemble more delicately. With the three instruments murmuring and whispering together, the coda is of a rare and shadowy beauty. It's possible that this was the inspiration to Brahms for the third movement of his Symphony No. 3, which has a similar gait. The finale is built on uncharacteristically dry thematic material and, like the first movement, handled with too much joyless counterpoint.

Dating from 1851, the little-heard Trio No. 3 in G Minor, Op. 110, has its moments, mostly in the opening movement. Here, in delicate textures and an unfussy sonata structure, the composer limns a consistently anxious mood. There's some interesting, pointillist writing for piano in detached notes against plucked strings and the coda, which, like its predecessors in the piano trios, accelerates to the end. The composer raises, then lowers the dynamics in distinctly articulated phrases for the three instruments. It's mostly downhill from there, however. The slow movement is an unrelentingly thick three-part exercise with unmemorable tunes in the outer parts contrasting with a vigorous, proto-Brahmsian central passage. The scherzo is built on a grayish, foursquare theme that's repeated obsessively, with a contrasting but still unengaging lyrical middle section. In the finale, Schumann seeks a happier affect, perhaps striving for what he achieved in the finale of the Piano Quintet. But instead of energy and joy, there's an excess of fussy country dancelike material, repeated and developed unimaginatively.

There's another work for piano trio from 1842, Schumann's "chamber music year." The *Fantasiestücke* (yet another set titled "Fantasy Pieces"), Op. 88, begun late that year, have more of the composer's early, fantastical style, and are worth hearing. As in most of Schumann's chamber works, textures are on the heavy side, and the piano dominates. But the four constituent pieces are loosely organized in a pleasantly relaxed way, and the titles have a comforting, Schumannesque ring: the first, *Romanze*, is a lilting barcarolle with a mock melancholy affect. It's the shortest of the four but quickly puts the listener in a receptive state of mind. The second, another *Humoreske*, is the longest and least organized, consisting of a spiky and playful main interspersed with episodes of contrasting character, several of which are quite beautiful. *Duett*, the title of the third piece, seems puzzling for a three-instrument ensemble. But you'll get it when you hear the violin and cello exchanging the tender phrases of a long melody, styled like a vocal duet with piano accompaniment. The final piece, *Im Marsch-Tempo*—"In March Tempo," seems like another tired, obsessively foursquare march theme. But you'll soon realize that the stormy mood of the march is not genuine but satirical. The interludes are charming and pretty and the dreamy coda is more than pretty.

The *Fünf Stücke in Volkston*—"Five Pieces in Folk Style"—for cello and piano, Op. 102, dates from 1851 but looks back in some ways to the composer's earlier narrative styles in addition to the folk influence mentioned in the title. Relatively small in scale, these are good for late Schumann. The first is a dancelike piece with some curious rhythmic hiccups; the second, a tender, very Germanic lullaby. The third is has a proud, ceremonial feel that looks back to "Important event" from the *Kinderszenen*, Op. 15. Third of the five sounds like a mock-heroic narrative, which again resembles earlier works, with the "Fable" from the Op. 12 *Fantasiestücke* a likely ancestor. The beautiful, liedlike fifth sounds like a nineteenth-century German composer's idea of a medieval ballad. While nothing you'll need to hear every day, the *Fünf Stücke* do make for decent occasional listening. Also from 1851 are three little-known works for viola and piano, the *Märchenbilder*—"Fairy-Tale Pictures"—Op. 113, similar in mood, structure, and charm to the five for cello and piano.

Sonata for Violin and Piano in A Minor, Op. 105
Sonata for Violin and Piano in D Minor, Op. 121
"F.A.E." Sonata

Schumann wrote two full sonatas for violin and piano in 1851. The curiously titled "F.A.E." is a work from 1853 to which Schumann, Brahms, and the forgotten composer Albert Dietrich contributed individual movements. Schumann's own sonatas are technically well made but betray the lack of personality typical in bigger, more formal works from this phase of his career. The three-movement Op. 105 consists of two stormy outer movements that are hard to play and entertaining to hear as they pass but don't stick with you; there's no underlying passion to justify the storminess. The most interesting section is the second movement, which hovers curiously and rather boldly between scherzo and slow movement. The more ambitious Op. 121 contains echoes of Bach and Beethoven, but without their expressive power. The long first movement, for example, opens with a contrapuntal passage in a dotted (long-short) rhythm and contrapuntal writing that refers openly to Bach's works for solo violin. And the main theme begins with slashing chords reminiscent of Beethoven's Sonata for Violin and Piano, Op. 47, nicknamed the "Kreutzer." Beethoven's expression in that work is fierce and terrifying, whereas Schumann's here no more than gestural. The remainder of this long, serious, technically polished sonata is, like its companion at once listenable and forgettable. Both contain lots of busy, carefully assembled notes with little impact. The "F.A.E." title refers to the initial letters of the words *frei aber einsam*—German for "free but lonely." This was the personal motto of the violinist Joseph Joachim, Schumann's (and Brahms's) friend, at a time when people still had personal mottoes. As mentioned, the work is an 1853 collaboration between Albert Dietrich, who wrote the first movement; Brahms, who contributed the scherzo; and Schumann, who wrote the slow movement and the finale. The melody of Schumann's brief slow movement is long, ripe, and pretty; the finale is busy and difficult, but again with no affective force.

Chamber Music for Winds

Chamber works for wind instruments make a refreshing change from the intense sound of strings that dominates the genre. While often lighter in tone, there's a beautiful and impressive repertory of chamber works for woodwinds and the French horn, a brass instrument that's commonly grouped with the woodwinds. The greatest chamber works for winds are Mozart's, but Schumann made a few pleasing contributions as well.

The Adagio and Allegro for Horn and Piano, Op. 70, dates from 1849. It's a well-made if not particularly memorable two-part exercise. The opening section consists of a long, graceful melody for the horn that makes demands on the player's legato, the Italian word describing the tying together of notes into a seamless melodic line, and a major test for horn players. The second part is an openly virtuosic, quick-time rondo.

The Three *Fantasiestücke* for Clarinet and Piano, Op. 73, also dating from 1849, seem more appealing. This may be due to the mellow sound of the clarinet as well as to their varied moods. The first is sweetly melancholy, the second tender and lyrical, and the last exultant. Set in straightforward three-part form, these seem unpretentious but are in fact exquisitely made, showing the later Schumann at his best.

No less charming and beautiful are the *Drei Romanzen*—"Three Romances"—for Oboe and Piano, Op. 94, also from 1849. The oboe's piercing, nasal timbre is refreshing, and the instrument sings more sweetly in its higher register. More than Op. 73, these resemble folk songs, with the sense that lyrics are pushing through in the eloquent melodies, all of which have clear, verselike structures. The third features a speechlike middle section.

Dating from 1853, Schumann's last chamber work is one last dip into folklike material. The bristly title of the *Märchenerzählungen*, Op. 132, means "Narrator of Fairy Tales." These four short pieces are set for a mellow ensemble consisting of piano, clarinet, and viola. Although from a time of the composer's deteriorating mental health, they're untroubled and sweet. Much like the works in similar style—the *Fünf Stücke in Volkston*, the *Drei Romanzen*, Op. 94, and the *Märchenbilder*, Op. 113—each of the four has a narrative tone and clear structure, a fairy tale told musically. Any and all of these down-to-earth folk studies have more character and appeal than do the violin sonatas.

6 The Four Symphonies, a Stray Symphonic Work, Three Concert Overtures

Schumann completed four symphonies, all well known and loved, each with more than one hundred recorded performances on the market, plus additional versions online. There's a fifth work, the Overture, Scherzo, and Finale, Op. 52, that's much like a symphony, albeit one without a slow movement; and we'll also look briefly at the three little-known dramatic overtures written for symphony orchestra.

The four symphonies are all works of the composer's maturity, with all the baggage that connotes. But the symphonic form, considered during Schumann's lifetime the highest in abstract music, drew him from early on, and he made several other attempts starting at least as early as 1832 that went uncompleted; he may have begun and abandoned more than are known about over his lifetime. Admirers of Schumann's early works for keyboard, including Franz Liszt, urged him to take on the larger, more esteemed forms for chamber ensembles and orchestra.[1] By 1840, Schumann was justifiably confident as a musician and composer. And with the new found sense of stability, however illusory, once he and Clara married that year, he took on symphonic composition in 1841, followed by works for chamber ensembles in 1842.

As we know, it was Schumann who brought Schubert's Symphony No. 9 to the attention of the musical world. By far the longest and most ambitious of that master's symphonies, the Ninth inspired Schumann to find a way to fuse Schubert's lyricism with Beethoven's structural rigor and work them into his own idealized style. As with chamber music, Beethoven's symphonies were a terrifying challenge as well as an inspiration to serious composers in the nineteenth century. While none of Schumann's four is as long as Schubert's Ninth, Schumann worked hard in all five symphonic compositions to find his own way. How well he succeeded is a matter of opinion, but certainly the structures and moods of all four symphonies are different and original, as is that of the three-movement Op. 52.

Both Schubert and Schumann served as models for later symphonic composers, including Brahms, and the Austrians Anton Bruckner and Gustav Mahler, all of whom experimented with form, stretching the symphonic fabric. The conservative Brahms remained closest to traditional forms and proportions. Bruckner's nine symphonies are famously long—long-winded to some; while four of Mahler's ten contain five movements, with his immense Third Symphony an overflowing six. These descended from Beethoven's longer symphonies, notably the Third—the "Eroica"—and the Ninth, as well as Schubert's Ninth and Wagner's operas. Schumann's symphonies are all tightly structured with none running longer than thirty-five minutes, and were not behind the increasing length of works that followed. Schumann's influence on Mahler can be heard in the five movement form of his Third, and in the rustic character of his scherzos, which Bruckner and Mahler both adopted and expanded on.

To all this gigantism there came, inevitably, a sharp reaction among later composers. By the early twentieth century, musical sprawl had begun to tire, and the noble classical forms were no longer viewed as sacred. Debussy, Ravel, Schoenberg, and Webern, among others, showed the integrity and force of smaller forms. Chopin's seconds-long visionary Preludes, Op. 28, were much admired, as were the wildness and radical fragmentations of early Schumann. With Stravinsky, rhythm became an equal to melody. That composer also shrank the size of his own orchestral forces from the huge scoring of his great early ballets to carefully numbered ensembles of the 1920s and after, with their sound deliberately altered from sumptuous to hard and dry.

Schumann's four published symphonies span ten years of his creative life, from 1841, when the First (the "Spring" Symphony) and the first version of the Fourth were conceived, to 1851 when he revised the work now numbered as the Fourth. The Second, a testament of struggle, was begun in 1845 and finished the following year; some hear it as a document of the composer's mental and physical ailments of 1844. Its powerful first movement at least betrays a Beethoven-like sense of conflict. The Symphony No. 3 ("Rhenish") was written in 1850. It's a work of high spirit and originality that also displays many of the composer's flaws in technique and lapses in judgment. The most consistently good and original is perhaps the Fourth, where the high thematic quality and energy of Schumann's early phase is developed over the course of a tightly structured, thirty-minute playing time. The Fourth shows the composer's high invention matched by discipline; its chief flaw is the heavy-handed orchestration.

In all four symphonies there's certainly more than enough fine material to offset Schumann's weaknesses. But one particular weakness has been long and widely recognized, and requires explanation. Many professionals complain that his orchestral writing has a uniformity resulting in dullness, a trait that seems more pronounced as his career progressed. Schumann often fails to change his orchestral texture, a procedure usually accomplished by shifting material between instrumental groups. It's a surprising flaw, considering that he had the work of his predecessors, notably Haydn, Mozart, and Beethoven, to study. He also knew and admired the orchestral writing of his contemporaries Berlioz and Mendelssohn, both of whom possessed this skill. For most listeners Schumann is a greater composer than Mendelssohn. But he's still inferior as an orchestrator.

Unlike his suites of short, highly colored piano suites, the classical symphonic movements on which Schumann's are modeled are long and broadly structured. As we've seen, those early keyboard works are vivid partly because of the brevity of the sections and their often fragmentary structure, where a two-minute panel might be crammed with three or more ideas, with each section differing from the ones that surround it, as well. But like chamber works based on classical models, symphonies don't work that way. Even if there's a contrasting introduction and an exciting coda, a sonata form movement—whether for piano, piano trio, or orchestra—comes in three parts: an exposition where themes are presented, a development where they are redistributed, and a recapitulation where everything is reexamined in more or less original state, if from a different perspective. Thematic material that's subjected to these processes is necessarily more neutral. Those tiny, brightly colored sections of *Carnaval* only work in that singular setting, not as seeds for the structural and developmental demands of sonata form.

These large sonata-form sections require different ways of varying repetitions of material, which an orchestra offers abundantly. Most symphonic writers learn early to shift between instrumental groups, taking advantage of the natural diversity of their timbres. To pick a well-known example, the first movement of Beethoven's Symphony No. 7 opens with a very long introduction, where string and wind writing are clearly distinguished, with the strings providing rhythmic structure while the winds intone a lyrical phrase. Then the strings play rising scales in detached notes as the winds provide the harmonic background in long-held chords that contrast with the busy motion of the strings. During the first movement's exposition, a rising three-note figure is alternated between the string basses and, in sequence, the oboe, the clarinet, the oboe again, and the flute. Even in the uproarious finale, Beethoven treats the instrumental groups individually, using the orchestra as a means of developing his pithy, mottolike phrases. Beethoven is considered a good but not exceptional orchestrator in the class of Mozart, Wagner, Berlioz, or Ravel, yet even he moves his material continually among the instruments. And this, bafflingly, is what Schumann seems to do less of than any important composer who had the resources of all those instruments at his disposal. The development section of the Second Symphony's first movement contains page after page where all the strings, woodwinds, and the French horns play at the same time, if not necessarily the identical material. The result is a uniformly muddy sound that could easily have been opened, brightened, and clarified. This is not to suggest that the symphonies aren't good, just that they'd be better if Schumann had applied this common technique.

Schumann's method of making different instruments share the same material is called doubling. Composer Gustav Mahler was also one of the most famous conductors of his time. Mahler loved Schumann's symphonies, but as a working conductor, composer, and gifted orchestrator, saw their weaknesses. The most notable of these is surely Schumann's habitual doubling. Mahler reorchestrated Schumann's symphonies fairly extensively, cutting, thinning the textures and giving thematic material greater prominence. Unfortunately, Mahler did these only for his own use, never publishing his versions. Even in an age like ours where textual authenticity and creators' original wishes are fetishized, Mahler's alterations would surely be useful for professional musicians to see and audiences to hear.[2] It's certain that other conductors have made cuts for their performances, too. Schumann's four symphonies all display his high energy and inventiveness, but are undeniably flawed by their thick orchestration. They are enjoyable on first hearing and fun to get to know. But for some listeners those heavy textures eventually detract from their appeal.

Symphony No. 1 in B-flat Major, Op. 38 ("Spring")

Schumann composed this well-known and popular work in 1841. Aware of the shadow cast by great predecessors in the symphonic field, he was eager to get one under his own belt. Clara, too, pushed him to take on the larger scale and theoretically nobler classical forms. In a burst of manic energy remarkable even for Schumann, the "Spring" Symphony was sketched fully in four days, from January 23 to 26.[3] Schumann himself picked the nickname, planning at first to give each of the four movements programmatic titles, an idea he soon dropped. While they are filled with good material, his lack of skill as an orchestrator is evident from early on. In case you're listening for the first time, the composer's other weaknesses including foursquare phrasing and rhythmic inflexibility are also present. On the positive side are the exuberance, warmth, and thematic fertility of his early period. The "Spring" Symphony is wonderfully exciting and inventive, but it's far from subtle. Listeners who prefer lighter musical structure and textures may find its charms wear thin quickly.

A proclamatory phrase in a slow tempo and rigid rhythmic guise seems to paint a stern winter out of which the springlike buoyancy of the main body of the movement will emerge. The majestic qualities of the opening phrase are played out in this brief but impressive introduction. Trembling strings suggest a shivering cold, and the stiff rhythm will later be transformed into a quicker, more dancelike version in the main section. More cheerful phrases from the flutes and oboes signal a thaw, and Schumann gradually ratchets up the tempo. A chunky call for the horns shows greater energy, leading into the main theme, roared out by the full orchestra. As noted, it's the opening theme transformed into a country dance. The composer hammers at the heavily accented (long-*short*-long-long-long) theme pretty relentlessly. The second theme, set in minor key and a contrasting rhythm shows a shyer charm.

Following the introduction, the structure is a straightforward classical exposition–development–recapitulation and coda. Schumann displays originality in bridging the development and recapitulation with an abbreviated return of the majestic introductory phrase. On the debit side, he instructs that the exposition be repeated, adding nothing to the forward motion that's one of the movement's chief qualities. (Many conductors sensibly ignore his instruction, moving directly into the development.) Another significant problem is that the orchestration is heavy almost throughout, with trombones roaring away, and the triangle chiming along, more than merely as an accent in the recapitulation and coda.

The linked slow movement and scherzo form the heart of the work, and may hold up better than its opening and closing sections. The second movement stands as a moment of lyrical repose in this otherwise high-energy composition. It opens with a long, rich, liedlike melody that's right out of the composer's playbook of great tunes. Sung by the violins, it seems at once mellow and heart easing. The composer keeps the heavy brass (trumpets and trombones) and percussion mostly quiet, but even here the instrumentation is laid on thickly, and the figuration that accompanies the melody is on the busy side. But it's all beautiful, and an unquestionable success. There's a contrasting middle section, with a mildly agitated affect that complements the tranquil outer sections. The woodwinds take the big tune in its last iteration; shifting the sound and mood is a quiet, choralelike phrase for the trombones and bassoons. An inconclusive sigh for the strings and woodwinds leads without pause to the scherzo.

This vigorous section is probably the most likable in the Symphony, thanks to the firm profile of its opening theme, a waltzlike ländler. Earthier than the waltz, though, this German dance opens with an instantly memorable melody set in a strong rhythm, as well as in a cheerful minor key. Contrasting tunes as well as two trios alternate with the main theme, which stays fresh on each appearance, thanks perhaps to a slight sense of ironic detachment. The first of the trios consists of phrases built on three notes exchanged between the strings and woodwinds that eventually open out into a longer scampering dance. Here Schumann again evokes Beethoven, the inventor of great symphonic scherzos. The second trio is built on a rising phrase played staccato by the strings replied to by chattering winds. And the composer wittily subverts our expectations for a loud cadence, ending with a quiet echo of the first trio instead.

He probably did this to set the stage for the flourish for the full orchestra that opens the finale. This huge fanfare presages the triumphal sounds and textures that will come later, but the first theme of this sonata form exercise is a quirky dance theme in Schumann's best, personality-driven early manner. The second theme is another German dance, sung by the woodwinds. These lead to a throaty climax for the full orchestra, which seems omnipresent from the opening of the development. At this point, for example, the trombones play almost continually to the end. But a slowdown leads to a shift to gentler exchanges by the woodwinds, followed by a faraway horn call, and a passage for the flute (marked "cadenza") that seems to show that spring has arrived in earnest. The recapitulation grows increasingly jubilant, with the whole orchestra (without triangles, at least) roaring away the whole time into an accelerating climax and coda based on the second theme, which initially seemed more retiring. Sensitive types who love Debussy should understand that the music is loud and aggressive for the last four minutes of this seven-minute movement. Here Schumann sounds a bit like Beethoven, as in one of the triumphalist codas from that master's middle period.

Overture, Scherzo, and Finale, Op. 52

Too long and polished to be considered a fragment, this three movement symphonic work was begun in 1841 but not completed and published until twelve years later. An indifferent reception at its 1842 premiere kept it on the composer's back burner. Lacking a slow movement but otherwise high classical in feel, Op. 52 contains echoes of Mozart and Mendelssohn, anticipating Brahms in spots as well. There's also a resemblance in its more modest scale to Schubert's early symphonies. Perhaps it's best not to overpraise the work, which displays its share of the composer's normal tics. Be that as it may, Schumann doesn't overplay his hand in Op. 52. The work is readily enjoyable if approached without undue reverence and performed with a light touch. The 1991 recording by the Berlin Philharmonic under Herbert von Karajan makes as good a case for it as possible.

A short introductory passage in a moderate tempo quietly sets a mood of lyrical reflection as several recurring thematic elements are presented. The first theme of the sonata form movement slips in quietly as well. Its short-short-long rhythm resembles that of the famously anguished one that opens Mozart's Symphony No. 40 in G Minor, K. 550, but here with a Mendelssohnian sparkle. Sung by twining solos for clarinet and oboe, the second theme has a melancholy affect. A thrusting motto for the strings first heard in the introduction reappears in the development.

The central scherzo is a gigue, reminiscent of the final number of *Kreisleriana* but without its menace. The rhythm is the same, but here the music skips along with a mostly good natured energy that's occasionally shadowed. Set in a contrasting rhythm, the trio, built of a noble phrase in call and response for the winds and strings anticipates Brahms. Also like the end of *Kreisleriana*, this witty exercise slips quietly away.

Larger in scale and more heavily scored as trombones join in, the more ambitious finale contrasts—not unpleasantly—with its relaxed companions. Working in sonata form, the composer introduces some stiff-jointed counterpoint and seems clearly to be in a more rhetorical mode. But the melting harmonies of the lyrical second theme anticipate Brahms, and there's a big, brassy climax that the younger composer may have learned from and reworked for his own Academic Festival Overture, Op. 80.

Symphony No. 2 in C Major, Op. 61

Although uneven, this big and ambitious work contains many moments of greatness, perhaps most notably in the powerful first movement where Schumann works successfully in an epic mode.

From a standpoint of musical history, the opening passage is a chorale prelude, a form much used by Bach, and the stern (long-long-short-*long*) rhythmic figure for the brass is the same as that of the start of one of the most famous symphonies of the classical era, Haydn's No. 104 in D Major. So, here Schumann shows his respect for two musical forbears. As you'll hear, though, the affects Schumann evokes in this passage are several and complex. The work opens in a troubled mood, which soon moves into a more heroic struggle. In the slow opening passage, bipolar ideas are played off one another. Strings and winds move in an uneasy winding phrase under soft tones for the trumpets and trombones, suggesting a call to action but at a dreamlike distance. This moves directly into a more sharply rhythmed passage reminiscent of Wagnerian lighting and thunder, against which the trumpet calls of the opening phrase become more explicit calls to battle. The violins play a tightened version of the sinuous phrase as the lead-in to the main subject, a thrilling and heroic idea in a sharp short-*long* rhythm, presented by the strings and woodwinds. The contrasting second theme is in steady eighth notes but presented in excited *tremolando*, a trembling effect for the strings. The struggle inherent in these ideas is played out in a long, agitated development which has the quality of a battle set to music, much as Beethoven put his symphonic ideas through their paces. The sense of struggle and agitation in this powerful display of Schumann's expressive skills is unrelenting and unrelieved. The only flaw is that of his orchestration, which as usual is thick.

Schumann's manic side is on full display in the scherzo with two trios that follows. The main idea, which consists of bustling sixteen-notes over an obsessive rhythm in a symmetrical phrase that's repeated over and over can be perceived as bustling or frantic. And sometimes the mood shifts unpredictably between joyful and violent, ready at moments to go off the rails. The trios offer welcome contrast with the fierce main theme as well as with each other. The first is a rustic call set in lilting triplets between woodwinds and strings, then back. Frequent slowdowns and accelerations also offer a break from the relentless rhythmic force of the main theme. The second trio also features canonic exchanges between strings and winds of an extended phrase. Soft, detached notes for the violas then violins lead back into the final iteration of the main idea, which is hammered out faster and ever more wildly to the end. Schumann adapted this type of rhythmically driving scherzo from Beethoven, and Bruckner probably copied both predecessors in his.

Set in two broad sections, the slow movement is based on a long-limbed theme sung by the violins at the outset, replied to by the oboe. It's a curious construction, opening in a distinctly mournful mood but lightening somewhat as it proceeds on its extended, twenty-four-bar course. This is because Schumann moves its tonality from a minor key to a brighter sounding major. What follows is a series of embroideries on this aria-like theme, some set high in the violins, others in scale-like patterns for the oboe and clarinet. A ticking figure in the strings decorates the theme, which is broken into canonic phrasing; the long melody returns for another full exploration, followed by a short coda at an ever-slowing tempo that seems to stretch into a lingering farewell. The instrumentation is light for Schumann, with solos for the winds, and the trombones left out, though a trumpet makes a couple of quiet interjections. Overall, this slow meditation is one of the composer's best on a large scale, made of beautiful material, and skillfully handled.

Perhaps the weakest part of the Symphony, the finale opens with a shout of triumph, kicking off a vigorous, marchlike theme. Some furious activity carries the exposition along, as several ideas from earlier in the work reappear, perhaps most notably the slow movement's mournful opening phrase. This sonata-like structure is a formal experiment with lovely moments in a sea of busy and sometimes noisy hyperactivity. One is a choralelike passage for strings leading to a sweet phrase for the oboe and clarinet. The composer tries to bring back the strings' sinuous idea as well as the motto for the brass from the opening of the symphony, but their reprise comes across as a bit contrived.

The polyphonic writing of the development and the climax toward the end seems another example of the composer's tripping himself up in counterpoint. Schumann loses control of the structure as he throws material together with manic enthusiasm. Yet when well performed this movement can be rousing fun.

Symphony No. 3 in E-flat Major, Op. 97 ("Rhenish")

The nickname refers to the Rhine River, on which Düsseldorf is located, where the Schumanns had moved in 1850. Impressed with the scenery and history of this western region of Germany that was new to him, the composer wrote this cheerful musical travelogue in the fall of 1850. Schumann's river is different in character from Wagner's myth-laden Rhine of *The Ring of the Nibelung* operatic cycle. Wagner uses the river as a symbol of a timeless natural world that transcends the strivings and follies of the gods, men, and dwarfs who populate the music dramas. Schumann's view of the Rhine is warm and humane, focused on the activities of the people who live along the river, though he is aware of the grandeur of the setting, as well.

Schumann broke free here of the standard classical format in this five-movement work. There is precedent in Beethoven's "Pastorale" (No. 6, completed in 1808) which except for a generally pictorial sense Schumann's work doesn't resemble; Berlioz's *Symphonie fantastique* of 1830 also has a five-movement format, but with even less similarity to the "Rhenish." Schumann makes his own use of the structure: there is, for example, no slow movement in a conventionally lyrical style, although the central three are all in moderate or slow tempos. It's an interesting and effective approach, and likely one that Mahler considered when expanding his own symphonies beyond the four movements. The "Rhenish" is a likable piece that has several flaws of the sort we've come to expect from Schumann in this phase of his career: it's thickly scored and frequently loud, especially in the first movement and the finale. Some will always find it just too hearty. On the positive side, the composer finds individual characters and colorings for each of the five sections and a longer, more flexible phrasing for a number of attractive melodic ideas.

The first movement bursts onto the scene proto-cinematically with the first theme roared out by the full orchestra. It's a long and impetuous melody, with a fine swing. Schumann makes it feel as though it's in midcourse when it starts, an interesting effect that's quickly clarified by a rhythmic compression that orients the ear. But he also miscalculates by staring at a high point from which he has difficulty finding his way down. The full orchestra, including trumpets and drums, is fully engaged from first to last with only a few reductions in texture, all of which come as a welcome relief. And the volume remains at *forte*—loud—or more for much of its nearly ten-minute playing time, one of the chief reasons why for some it grows tiresome. The second theme, a shorter and quieter phrase for the oboes, has great charm but its brevity compared to the main theme makes it an unequal partner in the sonata form debate. In fact, both themes have genuine appeal and Schumann achieves great momentum, but other aspects of his treatment could be better.

Schumann calls the second movement "scherzo" in the score, which his tempo indication—"very moderately"—belies. Like that of the "Spring" Symphony, it's a ländler, the German dance, this one with a more relaxed feel that that in Op. 38. The choreographic phrases here possess a more natural regularity than those in the first movement, but there's a memorable swaying motion here as well. This expansive movement is cut a bit differently than normal for Schumann. It's set in six parts, with a delicately stepping trio, a variation, and a development-like passage alternating with the ländler. Every moment is appealing and refreshing. Bruckner and Mahler have styles that are quite dissimilar, but both surely learned from and copied Schumann in setting generously proportioned rustic dances like this in their own works.

Schumann's tempo mark for the third movement is "not fast," suggesting an easy pace that's not too slow, either. Without leaning too heavily on the pictorial, the music suggests a rural spot on the riverbank. This most relaxed section of the symphony is also quieter and scored relatively lightly. Almost always heard together, the opening themes consist of a sighing melody usually given by woodwinds, followed by a delicately mincing five-note figure. There's also an easy-flowing, rippling sixteenth-note accompaniment for the violas and cellos, including a solo for the cello; worth noting, as instrumental solos are rare in Schumann's symphonies.

The most explicit tone-painting comes in the fourth movement. This solemn moment was inspired by a visit to the Cologne cathedral. Here the composer skillfully suggests that structure's grandeur and its dark, cool depths by varied musical means. Most immediately notable will be the slow tempo, the minor key coloring, and the appearance of three trombones for the first time in the score. Long-held notes also stretch the sense of near-motionlessness. Finally, a somber seven-note phrase suggesting Renaissance and baroque church music is treated contrapuntally. Here, the polyphony makes perfect sense, as does the scoring, which comes across as rich rather than heavy. Toward the end, there's an "amen"-like phrase for the trumpets and trombones. Schumann deploys ever-lengthening note values impressively in the closing passage.

Like a bookend, the finale echoes the bright mood and busy textures of the first movement. It's also as weighty as the opening, though more varied in its dynamics. The main themes are dancelike in feel, and Schumann retrieves several ideas from earlier in the work. There's a big climax for the brass that foreshadows those in the finales of Mahler's First and Fifth Symphonies. Schumann closely anticipates the latter, which is also that work's fifth movement, in mood if not length. But those who find the first movement of the "Rhenish" too robust are likely to feel the same way about the finale.

Symphony No. 4 in D Minor, Op. 120

Actually second in order of composition, this well-loved work was conceived in 1841, when it was also first performed to a cool reception by a Leipzig audience. Schumann then retired it, returning to and revising it extensively in late 1851. Contemporaneous with the First, the Fourth displays characteristics of the composer's early style, including vigorous and colorful material, cloaked in the thick orchestration typical of his later manner. Apparently the original version has other improvements and touches in addition to presumably lighter orchestration that would easily justify its revival.

The most unusual and original aspect of the work is its cyclical form, in which all four movements are based on the same material in differing guises. The variety of permutations the composer invents is remarkable, as is his sense of long-range architecture. If any of Schumann's compositions puts to rest the accusation that he's a miniaturist, it's this. Its flaws notwithstanding, the Fourth is overall the best of the symphonies, and one of the composer's most satisfying achievements.

The first movement opens with a slow, impressive introduction: a tone sounded by the full orchestra, followed by one of the work's main themes in snaking eighth-notes, expressing power and passion. A gradual acceleration, marked by interjections in the form of sharp chords for the woodwinds that will also play a major role through the work turns to an arching theme for the violins. This rapid, twisting figure forms the movement's strife-torn main idea. The nominal second theme is a variant of the first. These are built into a big climax, followed in the development by a triumphant sequence that presents a new take on the woodwind chords form the introduction. Although all closely related, much of the material is presented in the fragmentary and exciting manner typical of the composer's early style, with no more preparation than the occasional dramatic pause. Schumann plays these off one another with great power and structural freedom. He ends the movement with an inconclusive cadence in the major key (D major), but no retreat from the agitated mood.

The four movements are played without interruption, and so the start of the second movement, marked "*Romanze*," makes sense of the dramatic close of the first. Following a solemn chord, it's a memorable and poignant refrain sung by the solo oboe, which leads into the winding theme of the first movement's introductory passage, here muted and brooding, but still readily identifiable. The middle section of the movement shifts to a consoling major key, with a solo violin decorating the winding idea. The poignant oboe refrain returns to round out the movement, which, as before, ends with the instruction to move to the scherzo without pause.

The strong profile of this country dance resembles the scherzo of the "Spring" Symphony, but it's also derived from the winding theme that animates so much of this work's structure. Here the theme grinds along vigorously in the strings accompanied by an equally potent snapping rhythm in the rest of the orchestra; it's perhaps that theme's most penetrating and memorable incarnation, the likeliest to stay with you on first hearing. The same theme also underlies the mellow phrase that responds to this strong idea. Set in a contrasting major key, the trio consists of gentle passagework for the violins decorating a sighing phrase for the woodwinds. The composer reprises the trio incompletely after the second run-through of the dance, now with longer, tentative chords for the clarinets, violas, and cellos, which prepare the way for the tense transition to the finale.

This remarkable passage alternates dramatic gestures in a sharp rhythm for the brass with an eight-note winding figure for the first violins, all set against the anticipatory harmonic background played by shuddering second violins and violas. Chattering winds add excited commentary as the tempo increases, leading to a massive flourish for the full orchestra. The finale proper begins with a series of themes recast from earlier in the work, and some new material, as well. Ideas with obvious earlier lineage include the chunky three-chord sequence from the first movement and the eight-note violin figure, also mutated from the first movement's arching themes. A new idea is the exuberant skipping figure, set in the same rhythm as a number of Schumann's expressions of manic exultation, perhaps most notably the finale of the *Études symphoniques*, Op. 13, for piano. Here, too, the rhythm dominates the proceedings for a long stretch. But perhaps because liberated from the tight range and timbre of the piano, it seems to work better in this context. A heroic melody sung by the horns makes an unlikely first appearance during the development section, and there's also a rising theme for the woodwinds that shows the exultant rhythm in a softer guise. The remainder of the movement is an increasingly excited, accelerating progress toward a triumphant conclusion.

Overture to Schiller's *Bride of Messina*, Op. 100

Overture to Shakespeare's *Julius Caesar*, Op. 128

Overture to Goethe's *Hermann and Dorothea*, Op. 136

Great operatic overtures, notably the best by Mozart, Rossini, Wagner, and Verdi, form an extraordinary musical category. They set the stage, often spectacularly, for the operas they introduce, with many presenting musical ideas that are enlarged over the course of the music drama. Its cousin the concert overture, also called a dramatic overture, is a stand-alone version, taking its title from a stage play, but without an opera to follow.

Schumann's concert overtures, composed between 1851 and 1853, seem to be based on Beethoven's mighty models, the *Egmont* and *Coriolanus*, as well as the three titled *Leonora*. The latter were all written as overtures for *Fidelio*, Beethoven's only opera; their gigantic scope and power overwhelmed the stage drama and they were shelved. They all stand on their own, remaining favorite listening, as do dramatic overtures by Mendelssohn, Berlioz, Carl Maria von Weber and later composers, including Brahms. Like Beethoven's, Schumann's dramatic overtures serve as summaries of the action and musical depictions of the main characters. Each is a substantial work, running eight or nine minutes, and all are utterly conventional in their musical description of heroes, heroines, villains, and tragic outcomes, at least in the first two cases. (Goethe's play has a happy ending.) The overture inspired by Shakespeare is little more than a loud, brass-heavy march. A refugee from the French Revolution, Dorothea and her home country are represented by frequent quotations from *La Marseillaise*, the French national anthem, making Op. 136 the most readily appealing of the three.

Genoveva, Schumann's only opera, is rarely performed; its overture is the best-known and most frequently performed passage from that work. The most popular of Schumann's overtures by far is that for his setting for the stage of Byron's *Manfred*, which we'll look at, along with *Genoveva*, in the next chapter.

7 The Dramatic Works

There are three in this area, only one of which, the Incidental Music to Byron's *Manfred*, is a significant element in its small, self-titled subcategory. The other two are *Genoveva*, the composer's single, unsuccessful stab at opera. The third, Scenes from Goethe's *Faust*, is a problematic grouping of unrelated scenes from the great German drama, set to music by Schumann at three points over the course of his career, including his late decline.

Operas from the baroque era fall into sequences of short, action-free, lightly linked scenes in which characters reflect on their situations, rather like those in *Genoveva*. In the hands of Monteverdi, Purcell, Rameau, Handel, and others these are of unassailable quality, but they do follow different rules than do the more dramatically fluid operas of the nineteenth and early twentieth centuries popular with listeners and viewers today. (Retuning one's ears to baroque opera is not difficult, and worth the effort.) Be that as it may, Mozart changed patterns with his groundbreaking masterworks *Le Nozze di Figaro*—"The Marriage of Figaro"—composed in 1786; *Don Giovanni*, named after its title character, the legendary seducer Don Juan, written the following year; and *Così fan tutte*—which translates roughly as "That's How Women Are"—of 1790. With these, Mozart transformed opera into modern music-drama. For the first time, the librettos—the scripts—dealt boldly with real people caught in believable situations, and the music, from the overture to the last measure, was conceived to impel the story line ahead. Opera was never the same, though you wouldn't know it from listening to *Genoveva*, which bumps along as though Mozart never lived.

Every ambitious composer wants to write opera, but not all, and surely not Schumann, are suited for it. It's hard to pinpoint what kept Schumann from success as a dramatic composer. He was able to create rich ideas and tie thematic material coherently over long time spans, as we've seen in the Symphony No. 4, the A Minor Piano Concerto, and *Davidsbüdlertänze*, to name three examples of successful long-range management on the composer's part. And the songs are great expressions of complex emotional states. But somehow, he lacked the sense of dramatic urgency that makes opera tick.

Scenes from Goethe's *Faust*

Schumann worked on these three unsatisfying fragments between 1844 and 1853. Like everyone in and out of the arts, he deeply admired the poetry of Johann Wolfgang von Goethe (1749–1832), one of the giants of German and world literature. For many, Goethe's treatment of the Faust legend is his crowning achievement and in any case the most famous of his works. That mythical figure, whose earliest appearances in folk literature date to the Middle Ages, was also treated dramatically in 1604 by Shakespeare's contemporary Christopher Marlowe in *The Tragical History of Doctor Faustus*. Therefore, Faust was an old and familiar figure when Goethe took him up as a poetic and dramatic subject before 1780; in any case, he published his first play with the title in 1790. What's now known as part 1 came out in 1806, with the part 2 completed the year before the poet's death.

At the start of Goethe's part 1 Faust is a profound and brilliant old academic of high accomplishment. But he's also disappointed with how he has spent his life, yearning for the sensual side he's steered clear of over the course his own disciplined existence. Mephistopheles (the devil) appears, offering to restore to him time, youth, and good looks in exchange for his soul. Faust makes the deal. He then falls in love with Margarethe, often referred to by her nickname "Gretchen"; she becomes involved with Faust in crime and carnality. Gretchen is imprisoned and condemned, but her salvation is announced by Heaven. The wide-ranging plot of part 2 is much more difficult to summarize, but basically Faust is transported across space and time to witness remarkable figures and events, including Helen of Troy, with whom he has a child. At the end Faust, old once more, is dying; Mephistopheles tries to make off with his soul, but Heaven claims it instead.

Filled with ethical dilemmas and deep philosophical speculation, this tale of mythic scope has exercised an incalculable influence on Western culture and language. Even those who know little about Goethe or his metaphysical drama understand that the term *Faustian bargain* includes a warning that the bettor is likely to regret the deal. The influence of the Faust legend on music is enormous. There are at least three operas on the subject, from Charles Gounod's sugary *Faust*; to *Doktor Faust*, a rarely performed work completed in 1924 by composer-pianist Ferruccio Busoni, as well as Arrigo Boito's *Mefistofele*. The last, flawed but intriguing, is by the polymathic writer of the brilliant librettos of Verdi's last two operas, *Otello* and *Falstaff*. Poor Boito wrestled with his opera over a ten-year period. He was a better writer than musician, but listening to *Mefistofele* is a worthwhile project. Other takes on the tale include Liszt's *Eine Faust-Symphonie*—obviously "A Faust Symphony"—and Berlioz's extraordinary dramatic cantata *La Damnation de Faust*—again, obviously, "The Damnation of Faust"—which is probably the single most dynamic and compelling of any of the musical treatments.

One obvious appeal of Goethe's *Faust* to composers is that it contains quite a few songlike set pieces and musical backgrounds to the drama, including, for example, a chorus of insects in part 2, act 2. Direct invitations to musical setting include a witches' Sabbath, and a scene set in the palace of the Holy Roman Emperor, with streams of characters crossing the stage, singing. And throughout, Goethe sets lines for individuals and choruses, as if he expected music to be added. Schumann oddly selected only few of these, preferring instead the mystical, grandiose, and abstract in Goethe's poetry. (Mahler made similar choices for the second movement of his gigantic Symphony No. 8, which also uses texts from *Faust*.)

Schumann's setting is a compilation of unconnected scenes from both parts of Goethe's *Faust*, set into three acts of the composer's own arrangement. These were composed in phases, years apart, apparently with no thought that they would be performed together. The earliest to be tackled were the apotheosis of Faust, from Goethe's part 2, in 1844. Five years later, Schumann took up scenes with Gretchen from part 1. Finally, in 1853 he composed the overture and what form the second of his three acts, including material from Goethe's part 2.

Schumann was uncharacteristically unsure what to do with his *Faust*. The first two parts were performed in 1849 as part of centenary tributes to Goethe's birth. The full three-part score was not performed until 1862, six years after Schumann's death. The most consistent section musically will be for most listeners the third, but that also happens to have the least momentum. Acts 1 and 2 are really uneven. Again, it's unclear whether, and if so, how Schumann imagined his excerpts from *Faust* would be performed. As one might expect there are lovely moments, but listening to all three parts together in sequence is tiresome and disappointing.

The main problems with Schumann's *Faust* are its static feel and its weakness from a dramatic standpoint. Rarely heard compared to its companion works from *Genoveva* and *Manfred*, the unappealing overture is overwritten and uninspired, with foursquare phrasing. The material, consisting mostly of short motifs rather than long tunes, is reasonably good, but the composer's treatment feels labored. Three scenes follow: In the first, Faust sings to Gretchen in a duet that's tender, reasonably delicate yet ultimately conventional and tame. In the next, a remorseful Gretchen is praying to an image of the Virgin, confessing her guilt. This fine aria is both poignant and effective. The composer's attention to the character's shifting moods recalls his sensitivity as a writer of lieder. The third and final scene of Schumann's first act again paints a terrified Gretchen in a cathedral. There's a very long orchestral introduction, followed by the young woman's outcries, placed effectively into contrast with a thundering orchestra, chorus, and an Evil Spirit who is taunting her. Typically for Schumann, the phrasing is squarish, but it's well put together and certainly among the more dramatic moments of this uneven score.

Act 2 contains a musical depiction of dawn that's flat and uninspired. Many composers, including Haydn, Rossini, Wagner, Richard Strauss, and Ravel, have used this a chance to hit one out of the park with big effects, but Schumann's is very modest and unexciting.

The third part, composed first, shows some of the composer's inventiveness. Much, however, is also static, and highlights are few. The thundering chorus *Gerettet ist*—"He is saved"—moves at a quicker pace but is too long and seems stuck in a rut of repetitious phrases and a triplet-driven rhythm. Faust's death is preceded by a long aria *Hier ist die Aussicht*—"Here is the view"—that's supposed to sound rapturous but comes across as inert instead. The final scenes (the same set by Mahler as the concluding passages of his symphony) show the composer's technical skills and sensitivity to the text, but somehow fail to coalesce.

Genoveva, Op. 81

The plot of *Genoveva* contains numerous twists, but the story itself is fairly simple. In eighth-century Germany, the warlord Siegfried (baritone) is called away from his wife, Genoveva (soprano) to do battle with the infidels. He puts Genoveva in the care of his servants Golo (tenor), who is secretly in love with her, and Drago (bass). Golo, with the aid of his mother, Margaretha (another soprano role), attempts to seduce Genoveva, but fails. He then tries to dishonor her reputation, and nearly succeeds. Genoveva is almost executed, but rescued at the end instead.

Schumann's only opera, composed in 1847 and 1848, has never been well regarded and is revived only infrequently. Indeed, the work has many flaws, chief among which is that it lacks the sense of conviction that sells music-drama to the audience. The composer's treatment is dogged, earnest, and almost completely void of dramatic impact. The score chugs along word by word, scene by scene, and act by act with almost no sense of the architecture needed for a work of its scale; and, fatally, there's also no sense of the urgency that makes opera compelling. Schumann set the (bad) libretto with one note per syllable, with never a flourish or a repetition of a word, even for musical effect. Another miscalculation is that he fails to differentiate musically between the characters, whose vocal parts all seem to be at the same affective pitch and more or less interchangeable. Of course, with a talent like

Schumann's behind *Genoveva*, there are attractive moments along the way, but they come across as idyllic spots in a mostly dreary landscape.

It's fair to set *Genoveva* alongside Wagner's *Lohengrin* of 1850. The first fully realized masterpiece by that composer has a similar medieval setting as well as parallel subjects of sin and faith. But if you've heard any of *Lohengrin*, then you'll know it's incomparably better in every operatic sense. No Wagner libretto, including that for *Lohengrin*, is perfect, but here the composer-librettist understood and succeeded at his task of turning incident into a tragedy of mythic power and scope. Even though Schumann didn't write his own libretto, his approach amounts to little more than pedestrian text-setting. And it's surprising that the critically minded, literate Schumann set such a weak one. Even more important, Wagner's music takes up the argument from the magical prelude and carries it through the third act with unflagging intensity and beauty, and with only a couple of lapses of taste over its three and one half hours. Wagner's music probes deeply into the characters themselves. Compare Lohengrin's solemn injunction to Elsa in act 1 (*Nie sollst du mich befragen*—"Never may you question me") with the oaths Siegfried has Golo and Drago swear in the first act of *Genoveva*, lost in an indifferent musical stream. When the villains Elsa and Telramund open the second act with their plotting, the music depicts their repressed rage and evil natures with vivid clarity. And these are accomplished with relative ease next to Wagner's stunning yet subtle musical characterization of the ambivalence of Elsa, the work's tragic heroine. In *Genoveva*, by contrast, everyone sounds the same. As with many operas, the libretto of *Genoveva* contains quite a few improbable turns of event. So, for that matter, does Verdi's *Ernani*, composed in 1844. But that score is so powerful, passionate, and driving that we willingly ignore the silly aspects of the plot. In *Genoveva*, they stick out like sore thumbs.

Genoveva falls into an operatic category know as a "rescue opera." As you might expect, these involve a cliffhanger situation in which the protagonist is saved from a dire end, usually by an act of human heroism. By far the most famous opera of this type is Beethoven's stirring *Fidelio*, where a political prisoner is rescued by his disguised wife. Genoveva is saved symbolically by her faith, but the setup is identical.

Schumann and Beethoven only wrote one opera, but as with *Lohengrin* or *Ernani*, *Genoveva* is not in the same league as *Fidelio.*

Genoveva was first produced in Leipzig in June 1850. Although Schumann was by then well known and respected, the work was received with indifference, its flaws obvious then as now. And the high-strung, inarticulate composer conducted, which probably didn't help matters. Revivals have failed to establish a place for the work in the mainstream operatic repertory. Even among admirers of the Schumann's work, it's mostly referred to apologetically. *Genoveva* is by a great musician working in an uncongenial form, with moments of beauty that you'll find if you care to listen.

The opera opens with a long overture that strives for sublimity and achieves seriousness, at least. Following a slow, somber introductory passage, a more passionate sonata-form exercise follows. A number of themes from the opera appear, including an easily recognizable rising horn call. Marked by a dashing forward momentum, the overture stands well on its own, if not among the immortals in this category. It's followed by a foursquare hymn in an archaic contrapuntal style that can only be compared to its own detriment with the great example that opens the action in Wagner's *Die Meistersinger von Nürnberg*. Siegfried, the hero, then makes an announcement to interjections by the chorus that he's heading off to help the Emperor Charles Martel battle infidels, leaving Genoveva, his wife, in the care of his servants Golo and Drago. In the next aria Golo describes in conventional tones his secret love for Genoveva. The composer adopts standard operatic patterns with quick, virtuosic vocal writing following the slower, more tender passages. Siegfried and Genoveva sing a duet of farewell expressing their faith and hopefulness for his safe return. He gives instructions to his servants, then departs, to another chorus, alternately militant and pious, of his soldiers. This is a rare moment in *Genoveva* of the theatrically effective, as we hear their cries fade into the distance. Golo takes the stage, again expressing his desire for Genoveva. A flourish for the piccolos announces the entrance of magical forces in the person of Margaretha, a sorceress and, secretly, Golo's mother. She opens the final scene of the act with a quick tempo aria invoking the spirits. This aria and the heavy presence of the piccolos have both come in—rightly—for criticism. Perhaps Schumann was thinking of arias for Osmin, the villain in Mozart's *Die Entführung aus dem Serail*—"The Abduction from the Seraglio"—or Caspar of Weber's *Der Freischütz*—"The Free-Shooter"—where the bad guys are characterized to startling effect by that bright-sounding instrument. But those applications work, while Schumann's sounds contrived and silly. The scene and act end with a fierce oath duet for Golo and Margaretha that's too long for the text, plot and musical treatment it receives.

The second act opens with a lament in the form of a lyrical reflection *O weh des Scheidens, das er that*—"Woe for the separation he made"—for Genoveva that is beautiful and effective, like one of the composer's lieder. A chorus of soldiers makes rhythmic interjections in the background. Golo enters, bringing news of a victory in the war against the infidels. The two have an overlong conversation, but in the end, Genoveva asks Golo to share her joy at the good news by singing with her. This they do in a sweetly melancholy duet, *Wenn ich ein Vöglein wär*—"If I were a little bird"—that's modest but genuinely charming, and a highlight of the score. Overcome with desire, Golo speaks rudely to Genoveva, who rejects him, reminding him stingingly of his low birth. Their dialogue is supposed to be fiery but falls flat instead, probably because it's too wordy. Golo, now a fully evolved villain, swears revenge on Genoveva. In the next scene, the honest and shocked Drago is brought into the plot as Golo makes insinuations about Genoveva and the absent Siegfried in a long, dull dialogue. Golo persuades Drago to hide himself in Genoveva's room to verify her virtue. Margaretha and her piccolos are also enlisted to smear Genoveva's reputation, a standard plot twist in nineteenth-century operas set in the Middle Ages. Genoveva's saintly qualities are seen as she prays alone in her bedroom; this little aria *Du, der über alle wacht*—"You who watches over all"—is a pretty and pleasant, if fairly ordinary character piece. The darkening shadows depicted in the long postlude for orchestra are also well rendered. The big final scene, set in her room, is another operatic convention, a crowd scene. Egged on by Golo, maids, knights, and anyone else who might be interested steal into the bedroom. Genoveva pleads with Golo to defend her as he swore to Siegfried, but naturally he does nothing to help her. To the shock of the crowd, Drago is discovered. In the name of honor, Golo murders the hapless steward, though his goal is to silence the one person who can reveal the truth about Genoveva and his own false accusations. The text consists of standard cries of shock and horror, with Genoveva melodramatically crying above it all to Heaven for help. Musically, Schumann seems straightjacketed into ordinary gestures and square phrasing by the banalities of the libretto. It's far from his finest moment.

Heavy with twists of plot, act 3 opens with Siegfried on his way home. He has been wounded and is attended, quite improbably, by Margaretha. In the opening scene the two characters discuss his eagerness to return home. Golo arrives with a letter describing Genoveva's supposed infidelity. An orchestral accompaniment in a pounding rhythm depicts Golo's approach on horseback. Siegfried reads the letter in shock, then dispatches Golo almost immediately to return ahead of him and kill her. The music accompanying this scene depicts Siegfried's surprise and anger closely, at admirable speed and in a highly polished way. And the dying fall of the postlude is also tight and strong. Margaretha and a magic mirror are featured in the big, overcomplicated final scene; so are her ludicrous piccolos. She describes it in an otherwise admirable recitative. She then shows Siegfried the mirror, in which Genoveva and Drago can be seen to the silly accompaniment of spectral choruses singing offstage. The tormented Siegfried smashes the mirror, an act that deprives Margaretha of her magical powers. Now Drago's ghost appears from the shattered glass, warning Margaretha to confess all to Siegfried. The fatuous plot and text receive uneven musical treatment, with conventionally spooky and stormy affects likely borrowed from Weber. But the acceleration and fade down at the very end work pretty well.

Overburdened with coincidence like act 3, the fourth and last act opens with an imprisoned Genoveva lamenting her situation as she's led to the cliff where she's to be executed. Her two guards move to the background to allow the heroine room for her big aria of desperation, *Die letzte Hoffnung schwindet*—"My last hope fades." This long number opens impressively in a vocal line that moves almost grandly over a sweeping orchestral background. It may not be one of the great moments for an operatic soprano, but it's beautiful and quite effective within the flat context of *Genoveva*. Golo enters, telling her of Siegfried's order that she be executed. He offers to spare her if she will become his mistress, but again she staunchly refuses. Genoveva and her two guards, sing a fiery and interesting trio, *Umsonst versucht mein Mund*—"Although my mouth attempts," in which she tries to win them over. One, Caspar, wants no part of what's to happen, but his companion Balthasar says they must hold fast. Schumann's fluid treatment of the shifting sentiments they express is sensitive and one of the better passages in the score. The final scene unfortunately isn't as good. Just as Siegfried is returning and on Golo's order, Genoveva is tossed off the cliff, where she grabs onto a cross that happens to be there. Margarethe returns, crying desperately to Siegfried. He and Genoveva sing a modest duet that will never displace its titanic predecessor (*O namenlose Freude*—"Oh nameless joy") from Beethoven's *Fidelio* from anyone's memory or imagination. From here things move quickly to the end of the story, as Genoveva forgives everyone who has harmed her; a perfunctory chorus concludes the work. Schumann throws away the ending—something no composer with a real feel for opera would ever do.

Incidental Music to Byron's *Manfred*, Op. 115

Manfred is in some ways the most unlikely success among Schumann's dramatic compositions. Completed in 1849 immediately after *Genoveva*, *Manfred* is an interesting hybrid form known as incidental music. Predecessors in this small but important category include Beethoven's setting of Goethe's *Egmont* (Op. 84), Mendelssohn's to *A Midsummer Night's Dream*, and Grieg's to *Peer Gynt* by Ibsen. It's a flexible form in which spoken recitations from the text and music are freely interspersed. Mendelssohn's music-heavy version is of course well known and loved. Beethoven's great *Egmont* overture is familiar, while the full work languishes in obscurity; but it's well worth hearing.

As Beethoven's *Egmont*, Schumann's *Manfred* is best known for its overture, which is indeed huge, powerful, and impressive on its own. Also set in long passages of narrative and dialogue, *Manfred* has more in common structurally with Beethoven than Mendelssohn. Schumann also sets much of the text as musical duets and other ensembles, and in two bold passages, he sets spoken dialogue against orchestral backgrounds. Most of these seem, quite inexplicably, to work better than comparable numbers from *Genoveva*. Consisting of fifteen mostly short sections, *Manfred* is without doubt a peculiar hybrid, making wide popularity for the work unlikely. Fairly convincing on its own terms, however, *Manfred* contains some of the best music of Schumann's uneven middle years.

Starting as a very long, now mostly unread dramatic poem by George Gordon, Lord Byron (1788–1824), the source work of Schumann's *Manfred* was completed in 1817. Described by the poet as "a sort of mad drama,"[1] it was never meant for staging. Its brooding hero is tormented by an unmentionable deed and by the death of Astarte, his beloved. Avoiding suicide by a hair, he deals with Fate and other supernatural forces, dying reconciled to himself, but not to organized religion. The term *Byronic* has come to describe any tormented antihero like Manfred. And, although the poem, like Schumann's setting, is long and too obscure for wide acceptance, it has generated much admiration for a protagonist with a spirit that's passionate, self-questioning, and defiant of outside authority all at once.

Byron's influence on nineteenth-century musical drama was considerable. As we'll see, Schumann himself set many of his poems as songs. Two lesser-known Verdi operas, *I due Foscari* and *Il corsaro*, are based on dramas by Byron, with Corrado, the pirate-hero of the latter another typically "Byronic" figure. The same drama and character served as the theme for Berlioz's *Le Corsair* overture, while his symphonic work *Harold en Italie* is probably the greatest of any music inspired by Byron. Yet another musical setting of *Manfred* is Tchaikovsky's eponymous *Manfred* Symphony, that composer's Op. 58.

The original text is far too long for musical treatment. But Schumann follows Byron's three-act structure in a very condensed German translation, all prefaced by a great overture. Set in a modified sonata form, it opens with a scrambling that leaves us momentarily disoriented. A long, ever accelerating lyrical melody is then developed, then a more furious, headlong section. Hurtling chords alternate with rueful sighs.

Rumbling horns lead to a moment of repose in a yearning phrase, traded by the strings and winds. But the chilly sound of heavier brass enters ominously. This is the start of a strife-torn development section dominated by a tortured, twisting theme, followed by a return to the impassioned melody, here colored with flashing harmonic tints. Schumann recapitulates most of the opening ideas, leading to an impressive climax. The coda, introduced by the chordal sequence, ends, except for a few dramatic stabs from the strings, in a gloomy fade-down. Never overplaying his hand, ever-shifting in dynamics and rhythmic emphasis, this kaleidoscopic, fast-moving overture is one of the composer's best orchestral works. And if his orchestration is a bit thick, the variety of the material—and above all, the momentum—are so great that one hardly notices.

Musical highlights of the first act begin right after a long opening spoken passage. *Dein Gebot zieht mich heraus*—"Your bidding draws [us] not out"—is a delicate vocal ensemble; *Wenn der Mond auf stiller Welle*—"When the moon over still water"—is another fine vocal ensemble set to a falling theme similar to that of the *Études symphoniques* of thirteen years before. The haunting *Horch, der Ton*—"Hear the sound"—is an unusual setting of verse to a solo English horn.

Act 2 opens with a mellow orchestral prelude featuring playful woodwind solos. *Du schöner Geist*—"You, lovely spirit"—captures an elfin presence with a delicate use of the orchestra's high-pitched instruments. Schumann's handling of the orchestra shows a rare finesse. Known as the Incantation, the next musical passage *Heil unsrem Meister*—"Hail to our master"—is a spectral passage for chorus and the full orchestra. Rigid in rhythm and foursquare in phrasing, it's one of the weaker passages in *Manfred.* When he visits Astarte in the underworld, she and Manfred speak a duet, *Gerufen hab'ich dich in stiller Nacht*—"I have called in the quiet night"—over a long melody in the orchestra that's one of the score's most beautiful musically and original from a dramatic standpoint.

In the third act, Manfred has returned to earth from the spirit world which a stern, rather barky prelude for the brass depicts. Now more at peace with himself, Manfred sets forth his newfound tranquility in a narrative (*Ein Friede kam auf mich*—"A peace came over me") that's similar in structure to the Manfred-Astarte "duet" from act 2 in that the words are spoken against an orchestral background of great richness and beauty. For such a troubled man, Schumann had a gift for depicting calm. The final scenes depict Manfred's death, unafraid as always but now at peace. For this, the composer devised a saccharine conclusion that's out of joint with the spirit of the text and the character as we've seen him throughout. Manfred, speaking in German, bids farewell to a monk ("It's not so hard to die, old man!") while a chorus intones the text of the Roman Catholic Mass for the dead—the requiem—in Latin. It's a bad misstep for a composer so sensitive about words.

The peculiar structure and long spoken passages inevitably limit the appeal of *Manfred*. But with free and easy access on Internet, the purely spoken sections can be omitted and the moments of quality in the score readily taken in. There are many: *Manfred* offers unexpected rewards.

8 The Songs

Schumann composed more than 150 songs for solo voice and piano accompaniment; some of his greatest and most characteristic works fall into this category. Many are elements in what's known as a song cycle; others are settings of individual poems arranged in sequences as artful as the composer could make them and published, in groupings by opus number. Schumann dabbled in song writing as early as 1832, and composed in the genre as late as 1852. But the most familiar and surely the best of his efforts as a composer of lieder, or art songs, came in an astonishing burst of energy in the winter, spring, and summer of 1840. During this miraculous period, he produced about 140 songs. It's another instance of the kind of manic activity that's so typically tied with what used to be considered a mystery of genius.

Although Schumann's taste in selecting texts to set was not infallible, his wide readings and own skills as a writer made him an excellent and selective judge of poems. Schubert's seven hundred-odd songs would seem (unscientifically) to contain a higher percentage of mediocre texts. Perhaps foremost among Schumann's poor choices are the poems by Adelbert von Chamisso for the cycle *Frauenliebe und -leben*. Terribly dated in posture, they also seem like bad poetry, even to non-German speakers. As mentioned, Schumann had sufficient literary ability to cut, rewrite, and otherwise reshape material by less talented versifiers to make them better as poetry as well as to improve them for musical setting. With texts by Goethe, he rarely took such liberties.[1] It's also important to understand before we get to the songs themselves that no translation is ever fully adequate or correct. Many of the poems contain puns, jokes, wordplay, and other ironies that only German speakers can grasp.

Song cycles fall into two basic types: those that tell a story and those that don't. The first category is probably smaller than the second, but it contains several of the most famous, Schubert's *Die schöne Müllerin*—"The Miller's Beautiful Daughter"—and *Winterreise*—"Winter's Journey." The former, which relates in twenty short songs the obsessive love of a young apprentice, is the best example of the narrative song cycle. Opening cheerfully, a young apprentice tells of his love, which is never returned, then of his jealousy and despair; it ends, not so cheerfully, with his suicide. Knowing this great work is for many reasons crucial to a musical education. One reason is its subject matter, love and loss, which are probably the most common for poems used by composers to set. (Others reasons to listen to *Die schöne Müllerin* are to take in a folklike feel that disguises musical sophistication of a high order; Schubert's sure handling of its dramatic pacing, and the heartbreaking beauty of its melodies.)

The more common nonnarrative type of cycle offers many great examples. Like several of Schumann's cycles, Beethoven's noble *An die ferne Geliebte*—"To the Distant Beloved"—is so tightly woven that it seems to tell a story, but in fact it's a series of six poetic reflections on (you guessed it) love and separation. *Les Nuits d'été*—"Summer Nights"—by Berlioz similarly has a unity of feeling in its texts but ultimately derives its power and charm from of the composer's dexterous musical treatments. Wagner's *Wesendonck Lieder* also show the unity of purpose that, again, express the pain of an unrequited love; and they are also of high significance as studies for *Tristan und Isolde*. The best-known and most popular song cycle these days must be Mahler's *Das Lied von der Erde*—"The Song of the Earth"—six Germanic-orientalist meditations on beauty and its transience, but which, again, tells no story. Mahler composed four songs cycles as well as many lieder that represent some of his best work. Many more examples could be cited, but Ravel's *Shéhérazade* is another magnificent cycle also from the same era of high orientalism in European music as *Das Lied von der Erde*. Ravel's extraordinary trio of songs is unified by its sensual mood rather than subject.

If you go on to a more thorough study of lieder, you'll find multiple settings of the same poem by different composers. And sometimes there may be more than one poem with the same, usually generic title—"Moonlight," for instance. Influenced by Beethoven and Schubert, Schumann's own influence loomed large on later composers of lieder. The effect on his protégé Brahms is great, as you might expect. Gustav Mahler's songs also display considerable impact of Schumann, as we'll see. And Austrian master of lieder Hugo Wolf (1860–1903) also digested and metabolized Schumann's output profitably. Wolf's life and career also have several unhappy similarities to Schumann's. Clearly bipolar, Wolf contracted syphilis when young; destroying body and mind, the illness finally killed him after four years of insanity.

Most of the repertory of songs are, like the piano-oriented Schumann's, for voice with keyboard accompaniment. But as you can see, many other great text settings, including those by Berlioz, Wagner, Ravel, and Mahler, are for voice and orchestra. Other genre-stretching examples by Schoenberg and Ravel were conceived for voice accompanied by chamber ensembles. And in some cases songs written for piano accompaniment were later transcribed for orchestra. So, as you can see, it's a complex repertory.

From a purely vocal standpoint, Schumann's songs don't sound hard to sing. Their range is fairly narrow and there are few high notes or passages of showy vocalism. And clearly his noble goal is to put music at the service of the text. Yet many singers find them uncomfortable, needing transposition to keys different from the composer's original ones to make them more manageable. No one will be surprised to learn that artists tend to agree that the songs require considerable artistry to interpret.

In opera, we generally know which character is singing. But in song, that information is not always as clear, though it's just as important to determine the persona speaking in the lyric. Listeners need to figure out the point of view that's being expressed. Often, as in fiction, it's that of an outside narrator, whether it's a narrative, reflective, or as with some lyrics from the mid-nineteenth century and later, purely abstract. In other, very well-known examples, including several of Schumann's cycles and Schubert's two most famous (*Die schöne Müllerin* and *Winterreise*), the main character narrates his or her story. In some, such as Schumann's *Waldesgespräch* (third of the Op. 39 *Liederkreis*; see page 123), one singer portrays two characters. Several of Mahler's *Des Knaben Wunderhorn*—"The Youth's Magic Horn"—are written for two singers, which of course is helpful. However beautiful is the music itself or the voice delivering it, full appreciation of the composer's and performer's art require that listeners orient themselves with each narrator's point of view. In most cases the poetic persona is obvious, but I'll try to clarify the few instances that might be confusing.

Only one of Schumann's song cycles, *Frauenliebe und -leben*—"A Woman's Life and Loves"—is a genuine narrative. His greatest cycle, *Dichterliebe*, is not, but it's so unified in its message and true in its trajectory that it's natural to be surprised to learn the texts were chosen individually from a volume of poems by Heinrich Heine, and woven by the composer into a smooth, impermeable fabric.

The quality of Schumann's songs ultimately demands a full study by interested listeners and students. A survey requires focus on limited quantity, no matter how tempting the subject. For that reason, the bulk of this chapter is devoted to the five great song cycles of 1840: *Myrthen*, Op. 24; the two *Liederkreisen*—*kreis* translates literally as "circle" and figuratively as "cycle"—on poems by Heinrich Heine (Op. 25) and Joseph von Eichendorff (Op. 39); *Frauenliebe und -leben*, Op. 42; and consummately, *Dichterliebe*, Op. 48, also to Heine texts. The last, which is on the CD at the back of the book, gets the most detailed look.

Liederkreis, Op. 24

These nine songs to texts by Heinrich Heine (1797–1856) provide a promising start to the first of Schumann's 1840 cycles. There's a freshness to these that makes the set appealing, even though it's rather less familiar to audiences than *Dichterliebe*, *Frauenliebe und -leben*, or the other *Liederkreis* to poems by Eichendorff, Op. 39. Not every one of the settings is responsive to the words or message, however. As we'll see in *Dichterliebe*, Heine's poems sometimes open in conventional images or tropes, then contain one or more surprises, usually rebuking a faithless lover, toward the end. *Berg' und Burgen*, the seventh of these is one such, but Schumann passes blithely over the stings that are clear even in translation. His music is so delicious that ultimately it doesn't matter, but these are not always a flawless merging of words and music. The fourth song, *Lieb Liebchen, leg's Händchen*, comes close, though. It's a daring translation into music of every affect and image hinted at in the poem, and a clear model to Mahler and others as a bittersweet, folk song–like depiction of suffering and dread. And it's all of one minute long.

Morgens steh' ich auf und frage—"Every morning I rise, wondering"—is a reverie based on a poem that's more anxious in tone than Schumann's unpretentious setting. The text reflects a sleepless lover's desire and pain, while the composer's treatment moves along gently and sweetly. The piano line consists of detached chords until the postlude, when the signature theme taken from Beethoven's *An die ferne Geliebte* appears. It's the same rising melodic phrase Schumann borrowed and adapted in the *Fantasie*, Op 17. Here it ends the song in an open, inconclusive tone. *Es treibt mich hin*—"I can't rest"—is a strongly detailed study in contrasts. The song, which expresses impatience, opens with a fierce outburst by the piano, which the singer copies. But it only lasts a moment, as the tone of the poem shifts a bit; the end of the line is treated with a slowdown that approaches a complete halt. A closing phrase for the keyboard revisits the agitation of the opening. The composer changes tone completely for *Ich wandelte unter den Bäumen*—"I was walking under the trees." This slow and dreamlike meditation on lost love opens with a piano introduction of great richness. A slowdown and magical change signal the imagined reply of the birds to his pained question. And a reiteration of the keyboard introduction ends the song in a moment of stillness that approaches rapture.

In *Lieb Liebchen, leg's Händchen*—"Put your hand on my heart, my darling"—the composer sets a powerfully ironic Heine poem to the most startling number in this cycle. In the two-verse lyric a man asks his love to feel the beating in his chest, which he likens to the knocking of a "bad carpenter" making a coffin. The coffin seems to be for the persona himself, but (as we'll see in *Dichterliebe*) it might be for the love that's tormenting him. Schumann's folklike setting is deeply disturbing, and simple in appearance only. The piano and voice alternate, in a chugging rhythm that mimics the beating of the heart, but the composer unsettles us with strange shifts in harmony. Unusually, the piano ends first, leaving the voice hanging alone for the final words, *schlafen kann*—"so I can sleep." Any musically sympathetic but otherwise ignorant listener told that *Lieb Liebchen, leg's Händchen* was by Mahler would find little reason to question the misinformation. Homesickness is the subject of *Schöne Wiege meiner Leiden*—"Lovely cradle of my sorrows," the longest song is this set. The composer treats the poem with a blend of nostalgia and passion, all veiled in a freely flowing musical incarnation. The piano line carries the voice in alternating passages of long melodic and declamatory phrases. The sad closing lines *Lebewohl!*—"Farewell"—are taken at a slower tempo and there's a long, reflective postlude for the piano. Jumping moods to an energetic indictment of the circumstances that have sent the narrator packing, *Warte, warte, wilder Schiffmann*—"Wait, wait, wild seaman" has a convoluted text that must have been hard to set. For all its energy and literal faithfulness to the words, this lied seems less effective. Both the stentorian vocal lines and the hammering of the piano also make it difficult to perform.

The text of *Berg' und Burgen*—"Mountains and castles"—compares the treachery of the narrator's beloved to the dangers of the Rhine, on which he's sailing. But, as every commentator points out, Schumann ignores Heine's dark ending. Leaving that fact aside, the song is a pleasing depiction of the cheerful aspect of the opening verses. The lilting and graceful vocal melody captures the rocking of a boat on a sun-drenched afternoon, while in the piano part, which carries through from start to finish, we can hear the lapping of the waves depicted in tone. The music contains not a hint of the treachery, night, and death mentioned in the closing stanzas. In the brief *Anfangs wollt ich fast verzagen*—"At first I nearly despaired"—Schumann sets a lyric about enduring suffering to steady chords that reinterpret a Lutheran chorale used by Bach as well.[2] Ironically, Heine's poem is partly satirical, relating to the breaking in of new shoes, a double meaning that German speakers can grasp.[3] Perhaps understandably, none of this comes through in Schumann's somber setting. The poem *Mit Myrten und Rosen*—"With myrtles and roses"—expresses a range of emotion, including passions that are likened to lava flows. There's nothing quite so volcanic in the composer's treatment, the piano part of which rumbles along in a genial conversation with the singer. Except for the vocal line, the music could pass for one of the *Fantasiestücke* or *Noveletten*. There's also a quiet keyboard postscript.

Myrthen, Op. 25

The title, which means "Myrtles," refers to the tree whose leaves were woven into wedding wreaths. Just as Schumann's battle with Friedrich Wieck was heating up, the composer wrote the twenty-six lieder in the late winter and spring of 1840, with Clara's independence now possible. More than a mere dedication honoring to his wife-to-be, Schumann described *Myrthen* as his gift to her. Reflecting his imagination at its most ardent, the set contains many of his most beautiful and popular songs. The texts are by different poets, so *Myrthen* is a cycle unified by beauty and passion, but has no narrative.

The first song, *Widmung*—"Dedication," stands as it should with the most popular of Schumann's and of the entire repertory. Prepare to weep when you hear this one. Arpeggios sweep the keyboard, then the melody, a remarkable expression of a noble rapture carries in an irresistible tide the broad sentiments expressed in the Friedrich Rückert's text. For the middle verse, *Du bist die Ruh'*—"You are my peace," the composer moves abruptly to a cooler tonality and for the piano from arpeggios to solid chords in pulsing triplets. The vocal line gives the impression of an ever upward climb, with Schumann's radiant melody demolishing any and all resistance. Liszt wrote a lovely transcription of *Widmung* for solo piano that's well worth hearing.

The second song, *Freisinn*—"Independence," is a brisk and spirited take on a lyric by Goethe, in which a young man celebrates the big world he has just entered. *Der Nussbaum*—"The Walnut-Tree" is, rightly, another of Schumann's hits. The lyric describes a girl dozing and dreaming of a bridegroom beneath a tree. The flowing arpeggios for the piano immediately capture the feel of leaves rustling in the breeze, followed by a sweet sigh; the lilt of the voice and keyboard are interwoven with flexibility and skill. Schumann ruthlessly altered the poem, by Julius Mosen, to tighten the bond of words and music;[4] the result is magical. Set to a (translated) lyric by Robert Burns, *Jemand*—"For the sake o' somebody"—is a folk song–like poem with a carefully declaimed delivery. *Sitz' ich allein*—"Sitting alone"—runs only about a minute, but it's a brilliant setting of a cheerful lyric by Goethe. The persona is unapologetically happy to sit alone with a glass of wine. The composer captures in witty, jumping rhythmic figures the playfulness of the text. Readers who know Verdi's great operatic comedy *Falstaff* may find some kinship with this miniature. Another short dramatic monologue out of Goethe, *Setze mir nicht*—"Don't smack the pitcher down like that"—is a swiftly moving recitative that captures the persona's irritation at an oafish waiter, then the pleasure he finds in a younger, defter server. Like the preceding song, this flies by but is a work of big personality, and wonderful sensitivity to the words, opening in a blustery tone and ending sweetly. In *Die Lotosblume*—"The Lotus Flower"—Schumann captures above all a sense of longing in Heine's poem. The entire accompaniment consists of steady chords for the piano; a telling shift of key accentuates the rising of the moon for which the flower has been waiting. A curious poem by Goethe is the text for *Talismane*—"Talismans," a prayer and song of praise to a kind God. The rough-hewn quality of the text is what Schumann develops. The outer portions are in hearty recitatives with a more lyrical central part. In *Lied der Suleika*—"Suleika's Song"—a sentimental lyric by Marianne von Willemer (once attributed to Goethe) receives deluxe treatment in long, opulent melodic phrases interwoven with a keyboard accompaniment that could stand on its own. Burns's *Die Hochländer Witwe*—"The Highlander's Widow"—seems like a poem with too many words for effective musical treatment. Schumann tries his best, but the rapid fire delivery seems inevitably to come across as breathless and garbled.

The eleventh and twelfth, each titled *Lied der Braut*—"Bride's Song," are setting of poems by Rückert. The first is a sentimental farewell to the mother, which the composer treats with great tenderness as a sort of lullaby. It features a higher vocal part than much of the series, and has a long, beautiful postlude for the piano. The second is a brief but solemn dialogue with the mother, complete with pauses while the persona listens to her mother's questions. Although much plainer than its companion piece, this lied also ends interestingly, in this case with the repetition of the words *lass mich*—"let me"—that opened the song. This pair clearly anticipates *Frauenliebe und -leben*, written a few months later. The composer's energetic treatment of *Hochländers Abschied*—"Highlander's Farewell"—to a text by Burns captures the persona's patriotism and pride. The song also has an exotic quality that would become increasingly important in mainstream European music over the second half of the century. The fourteenth song, *Hochländisches Wiegenlied*—"Highland Lullaby," set to another text by Burns, is exceedingly regular in the fall of the phrases that make up this touching three-verse cradle song. The long, dreamy *Aus den hebräischen Gesängen*—"From Hebrew Melodies"—is set to a text by Byron. This seems as though cut from different cloth from the rest of Op. 25. Set in three broad sections, the song reflects the reaction of the brooding Old Testament King Saul to the heart-easing playing of the harp by David, which the arpeggiated piano lines in all three sections suggest. The outer parts are set in the piano writing and voice to phrases that wander melodically and harmonically, while the middle section (*Kann noch mein herz*—"If then my heart") is set to a beautiful, pleading melody and a tighter structure. This may be the most difficult element of *Myrthen* to get to know, but it makes more sense and holds together better on every hearing. The consolatory closing passage for the piano is one of the composer's most penetrating.

Rätsel—"Riddle"—sets a playful text by Catherine Fanshawe once incorrectly attributed to Byron. The whole song is based on a musical pun that only German audiences might find amusing, the fact that to Germans the note B-natural is referred to as H. (They refer to B-flat as B.) So, the appeal of this song is really limited, though as many commentators point out, the composer opens the song with a rattling B-natural for piano, giving the punch line away. Two songs, both titled *Venetianische Lieder* in which the Venetian gondoliers' songs are copied, follow. The English texts are by the (Irish) poet Thomas Moore, which were then translated into German. The unsurprising result is that they are pleasant but lacking in authentic Venetian coloring or effect. The first, *Leis' rudern hier*—"Row gently here," is given a lilting rhythmic treatment, the second, *Wenn durch die Piazzetta*—"When through the Piazzetta," opens with a sweet introduction for piano; the lied itself more charming than its predecessor. The difficulty with both is the chunky German language which never sounds right. Schumann's setting for *Hauptmanns Weib*—"The Captain's Lady"—by Byron is musically strong and effective, but more descriptive in its playful strength of the Captain himself. The composer's point of view is slightly off. It's good anyway, though, and filled with a witty mock militarism. A mild-mannered setting of Burns's "The bonnie lad that's far awa'"—*Weit, Weit* in German—features a closing commentary by the piano that's more affecting than the body of the song. *Was will die einsame Träne*—"Why has this solitary tear"—is a beautiful, melancholy setting of a poem by Heine that's universally described as mediocre. The piano supports the eloquent vocal line with chords that function simply from a rhythmic standpoint while adding harmonic richness. And again, the keyboard has the final word with a warm-hearted, falling phrase.

The cheerful *Niemand* takes its title from another poem by Burns—"Naebody," in the Scottish dialect. Here Schumann creates a completely happy fusion of music and text. In this brisk, straightforward setting, syllables and notes are tied throughout, and the melody has a real Scottish tang. The piano part is fun to hear, as well. Another Burns setting, *Im Westen*—"In the West," also shows great charm. This minute-long song is set in two verses, the first to sturdy piano chords that follow the vocal line. In the second half, the piano takes off in flowing arpeggios. The well-known lied *Du bist wie eine Blume*—"You are like a flower"—treats a simple lyric by Heine with fervent beauty. Pulsating chords support a rich melodic structure. Part of its undying appeal is its conciseness: both poet and composer have their say, never overstressing their points or outstaying their welcome. Schumann returns to Rückert for the last two songs in *Myrthen*. *Aus den östlichen Rosen*—"From the Eastern Roses"—is one of the loveliest of all, a fluid outpouring showing Schumann's tender lyricism at its best. It's hard to find fault with this flawless matching of words, voice and accompaniment. The final song, *Zum Schluss*—appropriately enough "In conclusion," is an overly solemn, prayerlike number that unfortunately destroys the poetic mood of the one it follows, in case you've been listening in sequence.

Liederkreis, Op. 39

This, the composer's third cycle, consists of twelve settings of poems by Joseph von Eichendorff (1788–1857), a poet who typically took nature and rustic life as subjects. Schumann seems to have composed the lieder that went into this set in the spring of 1840. The poems are unrelated but Schumann, his powers on the rise, wrote brilliant settings to all twelve and then arranged them into a convincing sequence with real cyclical feel and flow.

Schumann opens with the lament *In der Fremde*—"In a Foreign Land." He seems to recognize that the sentiments of the lyric are conventional. His treatment, however, displays ease with setting such a text. The restrained vocal line captures the melancholy of the narrator, whom no one knows or loves. The flowing accompaniment discreetly supports the voice and is beautiful on its own. *Intermezzo* praises a distant lover's beauty in an ascending melodic phrases over a syncopated, pulsing keyboard accompaniment. The speaker's rising excitement is portrayed in an accelerating phrase. The composer's ability to pair contrasting musical ideas in close contact is shown in *Waldesgespräch*—"Overheard in the Woods." This dialogue between a beautiful young woman and an admiring (male) hunter in a cold forest contrasts sturdy and more delicate phrases for both against a background of hunting horns imitated by the piano at the outset. In the ends she turns out to be a sorceress, who has trapped him. The song is ultimately conventional, and perhaps less than the sum of its parts. Those parts are certainly beautiful, though, and a challenge for a singer to put across. *Die Stille*—"Silence"—is a lilting, playful description of a young woman's happy mood.

Mondnacht—"Moonlight"—is the best known and loved of this cycle, and one of the most famous of the composer's lieder. The union of the earth and the night sky acts as a metaphor for human love. Schumann captures the mood of the text, tranquil yet ecstatic by means of skillful tone painting. The piano opens with a quiet note in the bass, followed a gorgeous falling figure from high on the keyboard that clearly evokes moonlight on a still night. Pulsing, repeated tones introduce the vocalist, who intones the words with rapture, as the piano plays the more flowing material and takes the more active role throughout. Toward the end, the pulsing notes turn into thicker chords. A leisurely, very beautiful keyboard postscript repeats the falling idea four times, each time lower on the keyboard. Even after the beauties of *Mondnacht*, *Schöne Fremde*—"Lovely, Distant Land"—holds its own. In another ecstatic lyric, Eichendorff describes the vague but powerful pull exerted by another night, this one breezy rather than still. The rustling leaves of the opening lines are what the piano depicts throughout. The vocal line is wide and restless, and there are more harmonic disturbances as well to capture the formless excitement the narrator describes. There's also a short but passionately beautiful keyboard postlude that's worth paying attention to. *Auf einer Burg*—"An Old Castle"—paints images of past and present conflicting. A warrior at a ruined castle on the Rhine is described as having fallen asleep at his post; meanwhile, life goes on and at a bridal party on a riverboat "a beautiful bride is in tears," a striking and disturbing image. Schumann uses old-style counterpoint and a slow tempo to make his effects. This technique anticipates that of the grave fourth movement of the "Rhenish" symphony, composed ten years later. To some *Auf einer Burg* will inevitably sound dull, but it does capture the message of the poem, where humans, their endeavors and sufferings, are shown as transient alongside nature and time. The following lied, *In der Fremde*—"Far from Home," has quicker movement and is marked by the repetition of a twitching figure in the accompaniment that suggests the rushing brook as well as the nightingale mentioned in the text, which compares past and present and ends with a desolate realization that the narrator's sweetheart is long dead. That phrase is repeated three times, followed by a sepulchral comment by the piano. It's an odd but haunting combination of affects and musical ideas that makes one want to hear it again.

Wehmut—"Sadness," the ninth in the sequence, describes the narrator's ability to hide that condition to the world. It's set by Schumann to heartfelt and beautiful melody that seems to go against the grain of the poem. There's a piano part that's notable for its richness; the composer sets it in three sections, with the fervent opening melody brought back satisfyingly toward the end. The text of *Zwielicht*—"Twilight"—is an allegory about infidelity.[5] The music of this striking song reflects a sense of dread. The composer opens with a long introduction for the piano in austere two-part counterpoint. The slow, steady creep of the notes leads into the recitative-like vocal line, which sets a tone of warning. The accompaniment is thickened gradually, and the final lines are accompanied by pulsing chords in the right hand. The linear progress of *Im Walde*—"In the Forest"—anticipates that of several songs in *Dichterliebe*. The work opens with cheerfully with a pulsing 6/8 rhythm that imitates hunting horns, benignly evoking the forest as well. The poet begins by listing standard country pleasures, such as a wedding party, birds, and hunters. But as twilight descends he finds himself frightened. Schumann captures both affects skillfully, never overplaying his hand in this short but impressive song. Both the vocal line and the accompaniment slow to longer notes as the evening chill overwhelms the narrator-persona. Twelfth and last in this cycle is *Frühlingsnacht*—"Spring Night," an ecstatic yet graceful lyric that expresses the persona's joy at the certainty of love in shuddering triplets that pulsate from beginning to end.

Frauenliebe und -leben, Op. 42

Schumann composed this well-known and popular cycle—"A Woman's Life and Loves"—to poems by Adelbert von Chamisso (1781–1838) in July of 1840, only weeks after *Dichterliebe*. A number of stylistic techniques, perhaps most obviously the commentary-like piano postludes that end all eight songs, with the longest following the tragic closing number. The poems track the emotional life of a woman from late adolescence, when she falls in love with an older man whom she eventually marries. They have at least one child, and in the eighth song, after the husband's death, the nameless narrator apostrophizes him, accusing the otherwise perfect man of hurting her at last. Schumann omitted a ninth poem, in which she is seen as a grandmother. The woman is not only younger than her husband, she's also from a lower social class and apparently less affluent as well. In the first three, she describes her future husband in terms that verge on worship; in the fourth, now engaged to him, she meditates again on his greatness and her approaching role as his helpmate. The fifth, set as she's preparing for her wedding, is primarily addressed to her sisters, though some hero worship finds its way in, too. Silliest of all the poems is the sixth, in which she reveals in the coyest way imaginable that she's pregnant. In the seventh, she expresses her joy at motherhood. *Frauenliebe* is, therefore, a song cycle with a narrative thread, an expression of one person's point of view.

Following these beautiful lieder in translations can be difficult for twenty-first-century listeners. Laughably dated in their postures, they seem clearly to be bad poetry as well. Chamisso's work came under criticism as early as the nineteenth century;[6] and in 1972 one commentator observes that "to modern taste, the woman in these poems is really too much of a doormat."[7] Others have defended how they stimulated the composer's imagination, perhaps reinforcing his own experience, pointing out that Clara was nine years younger than Robert,[8] and always deeply respectful of his creativity, which is not to suggest that she seems to have been a doormat herself.

It's certainly true that older texts reflect beliefs that are no longer held and attitudes that are no longer in fashion. But the decline of organized religion in the West does not keep anyone from being moved by Bach's sacred music. Operas put ludicrous words into the mouths of characters all the time, but again, there's no stopping listeners and viewers from weeping when an emotion is portrayed with cutting accuracy in glorious music that's beautifully sung to boot. This is how *Frauenliebe und -leben* needs to be heard: with all the tolerance you can find for the poems. Schumann's music speaks for itself.

Seit ich ihn gesehen—"Since I first saw him"—expresses in a carefully contained, almost prayerlike manner the wonder of the narrator, her sense of unworthiness, and her growth away from girlish concerns. The vocal line stays within a narrow compass, and the piano accompaniment, chiefly in chords set in a hesitant rhythm depicts the disruption of the patterns of the young woman's life. Similarly, Schumann inserts uneasy dissonances into the chords that conclude each verse. Although *Seit ich ihn gesehen* sounds plain on first hearing, the composer's treatment is a subtle, detailed character study that repays repeated listening.

You'll also hear how he brings the accompaniment back effectively as postlude to the entire cycle. The second song, *Er, der Herrlichste von allen*—"He, the finest of all men," depicts the woman's adoration in a more sensual way, opening with a throbbing piano figure that sounds like the pounding of her heart. The more energetic movement of the articulate vocal line, filled with turns and other grace notes, shows her excitement, as well as depicting her beloved's nobility of character. In one phrase, where she describes herself as *selig nur und traurig sein*—"blissful and sad"—the composer works in subtle harmonic shifts from major to minor, then back, as she resumes her litany of adoration. The pulsing of the accompaniment ends in beautifully twining lines for the piano.

Like the first song, the third, *Ich kann's nicht fassen, nicht glauben*—"I can't grasp, or believe it," contains subtleties that seem to give it more resonance every time one listens. Resembling speech more than song, this expression of the young narrator's astonishment and joy at having been chosen by the man she adores opens without prelude. Set against staccato chords, the breathless vocal line moves mostly in quick notes and in a narrow range. But changes in speed and subtle harmonic shifts underline her excitement. Just before the end of this brief song, as the singer repeats the opening phrase, both voice and piano take on a more mysterious wonderment. Now engaged to her beloved, *Du Ring an meinem Finger*—"Ring on my finger"—is an apostrophe to the ring the narrator now wears. The slow tempo and rich melody express her solemn tenderness. Midway through, the composer changes the texture to pulsing chords as the narrator swears more passionately to serve her husband-to-be. The opening melody returns once more and an instrumental commentary seems to put a seal on her joy, here revealed in all its depth.

Depicted in agitation and excitement on her wedding day, the narrator asks her sisters to help her prepare. The accompaniment depicts the commotion in her life in a swiftly flowing symmetrical phrase, while the voice seems to track her mix of happiness and pain. The latter comes from her departure from the sisters, with a quick dip at a slower tempo into a darker tonality. The composer works a bit of wedding march into the instrumental postlude. As noted, the sixth song, *Süsser*

Freund—"Sweet friend," is the most dated of the poems in *Frauenliebe.* For many, Schumann's treatment, which speaks to the depth of her feelings, is touching anyway. The narrator asks her husband, in a series of fits, starts, hints, and rhetorical questions why he hasn't understood her recent strange behavior. Set mostly as recitative and in a confessional tone, at a slow tempo to thoughtful chords and filled with hesitations, the woman, now a wife, reveals the unsurprising secret that she's pregnant. The middle section, opening with the words *Weisst du nun die Tränen*—"Now you understand the tears," is set over an accompaniment that pulses more quickly. The closing reprises the opening chords and slow pace. There are listeners who can't get past the saccharine text, and critics too who find *Süsser Freund* altogether contrived.[9]

Schumann's joyous treatment of *An meinem Herzen, an meiner Brust*—"On my heart, at my breast"—expresses the bliss all young mothers were expected to feel. The composer's treatment dances, from the two quick piano chords that open it, followed immediately with a rapidly flowing vocal line with a powerful waltzing lilt over swift arpeggios for the keyboard. The next verse is set to the same music but accelerating, and the final lines are set to even quicker staccato chords, but followed by an eloquent piano commentary. The pacing, flow, and mood of this lied contrasts utterly with what it followed and the grief of the closing number. In *Nun hast du mir den ersten Schmerz getan*—"Now for the first time you have hurt me"—the woman bewails her husband's death in a figurative accusation. Set in two parts, the opening is stark in the extreme.

Set in declaimed phrases for the singer, its accompaniment is only spare and gloomy piano chords. After her final word, there's a long pause, followed by a reprise of the hesitant melody from *Seit ich ihn gesehen*, the opening song of the cycle. So, Schumann uses the same method as he did a few weeks earlier in *Dichterliebe.* Here the recall of the old material also has a touching effect although by necessity it's a bit less consoling: her love is dead, while the persona of *Dichterliebe* lives and can still love. Reference to that great work will leave most objects of comparison in second place, so it's only fair to point out that *Frauenliebe und -leben* is one of the great gems of the vocal repertory.

Dichterliebe, Op. 48

Rightly beloved, this sixteen-song cycle stands as one of the high points of lied, Schumann's oeuvre, and music for the voice. Musical fingerprints—long postludes for the piano to nine of the songs, teasing, inconclusive harmonies, and settings that occasionally go against the grain of the text—will be instantly noticeable; these and more continue as strengths for as long as one knows the work. But beyond these characteristics, charming and intriguing though they are, are a delicacy and subtlety hardly to be found anywhere else in Schumann's output. The interdependence of the sixteen songs is also crucial to the overall effect of the cycle, but far from new to Schumann, as it reflects in its own way the influence of the multi-part piano suites of the early period. And ultimately there's a magic to *Dichterliebe* that words can't capture.

Schumann took his texts from Heinrich Heine, a poet of enormous popularity in the nineteenth century, and as we've seen the source of the Op. 24 *Liederkreis*. Written apparently after a painful romantic rejection,[10] Heine's sixty-five-poem set was published in 1827, under a title that translates as "Lyrical Intermezzo." Schumann adapted twenty of these, composing at white heat beginning on May 24, 1840, and finishing seven days later. Before publication three years later, four songs were dropped and the title was added.

Listening comprehensibly to anything, whether opera or song in a foreign language, requires the presence of the text and a translation. But even for non-German-speakers, it's pretty clear that Heine's poems are straightforward, without a lot of flowery language or symbolism to interfere. There is recurring imagery in Heine's poems; you'll hear much about flowers, kisses, tears, water, songs, dreams, and longing. But beyond these conventional poetic figures, and more difficult to perceive when looking at the words in black and white, are the irony and bitterness that underlie Heine's words, crucial to the force of Schumann's grasp of the text and to the grip of his settings. Schumann is alert to most of the affective suggestion the texts hold, but often what he chooses to emphasize startles. *Dichterliebe* is rightly celebrated for the composer's sensitivity to the words and ability to imbue them musically with what seems like every possible nuance of feeling. These sixteen taut songs, with the longest lasting less than five minutes and most much shorter, also make up a closely woven fabric between words and music, voice, and piano. Schumann also reins in his typical thick-textured, exuberant keyboard style so the accompaniment never overwhelms the voice. Individual songs are occasionally performed apart from Schumann's sequence, but the cohesion of and interdependence of each element really calls for hearing the set complete for full appreciation. So well sequenced and closely integrated are the songs that it's easy to imagine that there's a narrative thread; but in fact, there is none. The composer also achieves unity with falling melodies of similar profile in a number of songs. Perhaps the most remarkable quality of *Dichterliebe* is the seemingly charming flow that belies its deep seriousness. Schumann draws us along so easily that it takes a while to realize that the subject of the cycle is the pain of a spurned lover.

I'll summarize the short, pithy lyrics at the start of the description of each song. These have been adapted from the translations that appear in the Norton Critical Edition of *Dichterliebe*,[11] and those of Eric Sams.[12]

Im wunderschönen Monat Mai (No. 1 of the cycle and Track 20 on the CD)

In the lovely month of May, when all the buds were bursting, and all the birds were singing, love broke forth in my heart, and I confessed to her my longing and desire.

Forget the lovely month of May, because what Schumann unexpectedly focuses on in the opening song are the longing and desire mentioned in the last line of Heine's poem. The opening phrase for the piano is a sigh set to music; the deliberate tempo has no hint of springlike bounce. From a harmonic standpoint, the composer leaves the tonality uncertain here and throughout, ending the song on another unresolved dissonance, a bold strategy for 1840, that also creates a gravitational pull toward the next number. The vocal and instrumental parts are tightly interwoven, as the voice and piano share the upward reach of the melody.[13]

Aus meinen Thränen spriessen (No. 2; Track 21)

From my tears sprang flowers; my sighs turned into a chorus of nightingales. If you love me, then I give you all the flowers, and the nightingale will sing before your window.

Here, again the mournful words are not matched by the music, which is more reflective than sad. Schumann's melodic line correctly accents crucial words, notably *spriessen*—"spring up"—in the first verse and *klingen*—"sound"—in the second.

Die Rose, die Lilie, die Taube, die Sonne (No. 3; Track 22)

The rose, lily, dove, the sun, I loved blissfully. I love them no more: only the little one, the dainty one, the pure one, the wellspring of love, she's the rose, lily, dove, and sun.

An astonishing thirty seconds long, this song is a breathless listing of natural wonders that pale next to the beloved. The composer depicts this sense of wonder in a quick-tempo patter for the singer set against a delicately pointillistic accompaniment for the piano, featuring detached notes in the left hand below chords in the right.

Wenn ich in deine Augen seh' (No. 4; Track 23)

When I look into your eyes, my sorrow and pain vanish; but when I kiss your mouth, I am fully healed. When I lie on your breast, Heavenly bliss overtakes me. But when you say, "I love you," I can only weep bitterly.

Heine ends the poem with a sharp expression of mistrust that Schumann doesn't fully exploit. The tone of his setting has an almost prayerful quality, with the keyboard commenting in chords on the steady murmur of the vocal line. The piano part sometimes anticipates the voice, following it at others. A slight shift in harmony starting at the word *sprichst*—"say"—hints reticently at disturbance.

Ich will meine Seele tauchen (No. 5; Track 24)

I will dip my soul into the lily, which shall breathe of my beloved. The song will tremble, like her kiss that magical hour.

With not a wasted phrase, gesture, or note this may be the most purely beautiful song in *Dichterliebe*. An ardent melody carrying the text hovers above a fleet-footed accompaniment. To add impetus, Schumann places the monosyllables (*Ich, die, das, den*) that open the lines and stanzas of the text on weak beats that precede the opening note of the song's four musical phrases. The last quarter of this dazzling minute-long lied is given over to a postlude for the keyboard—an intense sinking idea, close in profile and spirit to the melody.

Im Rhein, im heiligen Strome (No. 6; Track 25)

The holy Rhine reflects in its waves the city of Cologne and its great cathedral. In the cathedral hangs a painting on gilded leather that has smiled on my wild confusion. Flowers and cherubs hover about the Virgin, whose eyes, lips, and cheeks are just like my beloved's.

Schumann varies the speed, textures, and feel of the cycle with the next song. The majesty of the cathedral is depicted in a dotted (short-*long*) rhythm, imitating Baroque musical forms that dominate the accompaniment of this song.[14] It's all slower, more deliberate, and thicker in texture than *Ich will meine Seele tauchen*. The composer softens the harmonies in the second and third verses, set inside the cathedral and describing the painting and its consoling effect on the narrator. A long instrumental postlude resumes the more severe tone of the opening stanza.

Ich grolle nicht (No. 7; Track 26)

I bear no grudge, though my heart may break, oh love forever lost. You may shine in your diamonds, but no light shines into your heart. In a dream I saw a serpent eating your heart; I saw how wretched you are.

The composer shows himself to be astute in his understanding of human nature in this well-known lied. Over pounding chords for the piano, the singer insists six times that he bears no grudge, even though the poem opens with those words, repeating them only once. (Repetition of words and phrases is common in vocal treatments of texts from classical to popular, but it's a method Schumann tends to use sparingly.) The vocal line rises powerfully over the continual throbbing of the piano. Much here depends on the singer. Some play it straight, characterizing the narrator as self-deluding in his posture of manly stoicism, whereas many sing it with the anger that's also clearly present. Both strategies can be made to work.

Und wüssten's die Blumen (No. 8; Track 27)

If the flowers know how wounded my heart is, they would weep to ease my pain. If the nightingales knew how sad and sick, they would sing to cheer me. If the stars knew my sorrow, they would come down and comfort me. But they cannot understand it; only she who has broken my heart knows my suffering.

Another beauty in the spirit of No. 5, here a falling melody of similar character is set against a shimmering *tremolando* accompaniment. Both voice and piano have lighter parts that differ from the two preceding forceful songs, and this moves swiftly and steadily. On the word *zerrissen*—"broken"—the pulse stops for two powerfully dissonant piano chords and a powerful and furious postlude that clearly recalls the surging opening of *Kreisleriana*. The rage expressed in the closing phrases contrasts strikingly with the delicate textures of what went before.

Das ist ein Flöten und Geigen (No. 9; Track 28)

There's the sound of flutes and fiddles, with trumpets blaring, too; there in the wedding party my love is dancing. Among the tinkling and booming of drums and pipes you can hear the angels weep.

The persona listens in misery to the music at his beloved's wedding. Schumann's waltz for the piano contrasts with another penetrating rendering of the singer's psychology as he lurks outside the hall. The composer, for example, raises the dynamics on the words describing the sounds themselves, which he then lowers for the depiction of the singer's pained reactions. This ironic and bitter song stood as an example to Mahler, who learned and amplified Schumann's methods. The postlude is again a long fade-down; the final bars were clearly copied by Mahler at the end of his song *Des Antonius von Padua Fischpredigt*—"St. Anthony of Padua's Sermon to the Fish."[15]

Hör' ich das Liedchen klingen (No. 10; Track 29)

When I hear the song my sweetheart sang, my heart wants to burst from pain. Longing drives me to the woods, where my grief finds relief in tears.

Schumann evokes the narrator's desolation in this beautiful lied. The tempo is slow and textures delicate; piano and vocal lines are closely interwoven throughout. The piano opens, stating a sighing tune over falling arpeggios. The singer then enters with the same melody; but there is no comfort to be found for his *übergrosses Weh*—"overwhelming grief." A somber instrumental postscript carries the mood of unrelenting pain to the end.

Ein Jüngling liebt ein Mädchen (No. 11; Track 30)

A boy loves a girl who loves someone else, who loves yet another and marries her. So, the girl, out of spite, marries the first man who comes along, and the boy is miserable. It's an old story, yet always new; whoever experiences it has his heart broken.

The unhappy contingencies of the text will make the jaunty and at times coarse qualities of Schumann's musical treatment surprising to some. Two intelligent performers have shown the composer's intent, however. The German baritone Dietrich Fischer-Dieskau (1924–2012), one of the greatest interpreters of lied in the twentieth century, sang *Dichterliebe* many times, recording it more than once as well. Fischer-Dieskau observes that the song "demonstrates Schumann's ability to do justice to Heine's sarcastic tone."[16] And American pianist and musicologist Charles Rosen probes even deeper. Describing the tune as "ostentatiously commonplace . . . deliberately awkward . . . positively ugly," Rosen shows how Schumann's setting "makes Heine's facetiousness more profound as well as more dramatic," and that it can only functions fully in the context of this cycle. Rosen also points out correctly that Schumann's irony opened pathways for later composers, including Mahler, Berg, and Stravinsky.[17]

The satirical force of Schumann's treatment can be found from the faux jollity of the folklike introduction to the at times uncomfortably high vocal line, to his straight treatment of the brutal punch line, made stinging by the very lack of sympathy in the music, which chugs along just as it did from the start. There's a keyboard commentary reiterating the introduction in which a new sense of irony, pain, and a proto-Mahlerian bitterness can be heard. As in No. 7, singers can and often do interpolate pain into the last two lines.

Am leuchtenden Sommermorgen (No. 12; Track 31)

On a bright summer morning I walk in the garden where the flowers whisper and talk. But I wander in silence. They whisper in pity, "Don't be angry with our sister, you sad, pale man."

The more spacious proportions of this song mark a slight shift in tone and dimension toward the later part of the cycle. A gentle, falling figure in a slow tempo for the piano sets a mood that's clearly less troubled. The dipping piano figure seems to depict the movement of the flowers in the summer breeze, and there's a telling shift in harmony as the narrator imagines the flowers asking him to forgive. The singer's long line has a gentle lilt from start to finish, and there's a leisurely, reflective, and very beautiful keyboard postlude, pointing to the even longer one that ends the cycle, to which this is the precursor.

Ich hab' im Traum geweinet (No. 13; Track 32)

I wept in my dream; I dreamed you lay in your grave. When I woke, tears streamed down my cheeks. I cried in my dream. I dreamed that you had left me; when I woke, I wept long and bitterly. I cried in my dream. I dreamed that you still loved me. When I woke, my tears still flowed.

For this grimmest element in *Dichterliebe* Schumann uses musical images that recall a funeral procession heard as from a distance. The singer opens, quietly with a confiding phrase in a speechlike rhythm. After a noticeable pause, the piano plays a drumbeatlike figure in the bass. In the first two verses the singer and pianist seem as though moving in separate worlds. Silence in the form of long rests has an alarming presence in the opening and closing sections. The third verse put singer and keyboard together finally as the voice rises despairingly for the final phrase. Two quiet, disconnected grumblings from the piano make a terrifying conclusion.

Allnächtlich im Traume (No. 14; Track 33)

Every night in my dreams I see you and your smile; weeping, I fall at your feet. You look at me sadly, shake your head, as from your eyes steal teardrops like pearls. You whisper a word and hand me a cypress wreath; I wake, the wreath is gone, and I've forgotten the word.

With contrast needed after the unrelieved darkness of the last song, the opening phrase of this lied opens with a rising melodic phrase that's wistful if not exactly optimistic. Schumann skillfully captures the vagueness of the dreams related in Heine's poem. Here he repeats words (*schüttelst*—"shake") for emphasis, as the narrator might in his effort to recount his dream. There's an interesting shift in the beat for one measure at the center of the song (the last two lines of the second verse) where the composer adapts to the more rapid flow of the words. And the open phrasing and harmony of the ending brilliantly captures the difficulty of recalling and describing dreams.

The last two songs are longer and more complex.

Aus alten Märchen (No. 15; Track 34)

From old fairy tales a white hand waves; there are sounds and songs of a magic land where flowers bloom with a face like a bride's. There, green trees sing old tunes, bids sing joyfully and misty shapes rise and dance to a mystical chorus. [. . .] Singing springs gush and strange reflections shine in the streams. Ah, if only I could go there and set my heart at ease . . . I see that land of rapture in my dreams, but in the morning it vanishes like foam.

The longest text setting in *Dichterliebe*, *Aus alten Märchen* consists chiefly of a list of fantasies that, as the narrator is learning, are as unrealistic as his romantic hopes. The pianist opens the song with an upward-reaching, apparently cheerful melody set in a skipping 6/8 beat. The singer enters with the same tune, described in the opening words as "old fairy tales." These the composer builds subtly but steadily toward a climax on the fervent words *Ach, könnt' ich dorthin kommen*—"Ah, if only I could go there"—the climactic moment of the song and perhaps of the entire cycle. In a long wind-down, Schumann slows the tempo and lengthens the note values for the recitation of the moral that it was all a dream that vanishes in the morning like foam. The accompanist sounds the melodic phrase that opened and dominated the song, now slowly and more softly, reflecting its hopeful sentiment but as though in fading light.

Die alten, bösen Lieder (No. 16; Track 35)

The old, ugly songs, the wicked dreams, let's now bury them in a large coffin. There's much to place in it, so it must be bigger than the great vat of Heidelberg, longer than the bridge at Mainz, stronger than St. Christopher in Cologne cathedral. They must carry the coffin and sink it in the sea . . . Do you know why it must be so large and heavy? I'm burying all my love and pain.

The final song is in two parts. In the opening section, the narrator, his tone mixing disgust, a hint of self-disgust, and manly resolution describes in a series of comically exaggerated metaphors how he plans to bury the old songs that torment him. Following a big, satirical flourish for the piano, he describes his decision in a sequence of titanic images, which the accompaniment energetically follows. These culminate in the fifth verse with chords that wittily combine funeral march with a heave-ho motion as he describes the coffin being sunk in the sea, the only place big enough to hold it. The tone changes for the final two lines, as the question of why so large a coffin is needed is asked. The hushed reply is made to slowing of tempo, and a mysterious change of key. Another change of key leads to an extended meditation on the postlude to No. 12. This marvelous passage, longest and loveliest of the *Dichterliebe* postludes, sings without lyrics—because none are needed—of consolation, a love that's still not dead, and of the redemptive power of love. Not needing explanation or analysis, it's the culminating masterstroke to the accumulating greatness of the cycle. Those who know Eric Clapton's 1970 masterpiece *Layla* will find a similar structure, with the lacerating pain of the opening part followed and tied, as though inevitably, to the wordless solace of the second.

Even though the original twenty-song version is rarely performed, the four songs deleted in the first published edition are well worth hearing. Charles Rosen commented, "The first and more complete version seems to me both more original and more moving"[18] and other listeners and performers also find the longer *Dichterliebe* an improvement. But by now the taut near-perfection of the sixteen song version is unlikely to be dislodged. Published posthumously as Op. 142, the four deleted numbers are easy to find online; you can then interpolate them and form your own opinion. Their first two, *Dein Angesicht* and *Lehn' deine Wang*, stood between the present fourth (*Wenn ich in deine Augen seh'*) and fifth (*Ich will meine Seele tauschen*). *Dein Angesicht*—"Your face so dear"—is a slow setting of a somber lyric into which death intrudes. The melody is penetrating and the accompaniment patented Schumann, with an evocative postlude. Setting a more openly erotic poem, *Lehn' deine Wang*—"Lay your cheek"—places its passionate vocal line against hurtling triplets for the piano.

The next two songs, *Es leuchtet meine Liebe* and *Mein Wagen rollet langsam*, originally took their place between the twelfth and thirteenth songs. These are longer and both more impressive in their way than the first two. *Es leuchtet meine Liebe*—"My love shines"—is another recounting of an ominous dream. Schumann's virtuosic, piano-heavy setting inevitably reminds us of the seminal *Kreisleriana* and other early keyboard works. There's a long, powerful closing commentary in shifting moods and colors for the keyboard. Perhaps the main problem with this potent and impressive song is the accompaniment, which comes close to swamping the vocal line. But *Es leuchtet meine Liebe* is surely worth seeking out. So, for that matter, is *Mein Wagen rollet langsam*—"My carriage moves slowly," last of the deleted songs. Here the narrator-persona imagines mocking faces in the forest he's traveling through in his carriage. Again, the accompaniment is remarkable for its beauty and sensitivity to the text. Set above rumbling bass notes, the delicate figuration of the right hand depicts the movement of the carriage wheels, trailing off into silence at the end. The proto-Debussyan harmonic haze powerfully suggests the narrator's distraction resulting from the hypnotic movement of his carriage in the dreamlike forest. In between, playful chords in a new rhythm depict the imaginary, mocking shadow forms. Schumann sets the vocal line mostly in long notes for the reflective passages and shorter notes for those depicting the teasing. *Mein Wagen rollet langsam* is a minor masterpiece on its own.

As noted, the cycles mostly composed in the first six months of 1840 represent a high water mark in the composer's song output, as well as a sizable percentage of the songs. And as you might expect, there are other treasures. But as is the case with every category of the composer's output, earlier is almost always better. Schumann had two later phases of songwriting productivity, the first in 1849 and 1850, and another in 1852. The opus numbers for the first of these phases—74, 77, 79, 83, 87, 89, 90, 95, 96, and 98—contain some items of quality, but nothing like that of ten years earlier. And the final lieder—anything in the category with an opus number of 104 or higher—should be approached with lower expectations:

> The evidence of the songs is plain. Schumann never again reached or even approached the level of his 1840 masterpieces. The songs of 1849 are a decline; the later ones a descent, first steep, then precipitous. . . . Other composers of comparable stature are believed to mature in their music; Schumann appears to deteriorate. . . .[19]

9 Listening to Schumann

As we've seen, Schumann is an uneven composer. When great, his work is as compelling as music can be, seizing our attention and admiration with ease. As a result, there are dozens, if not hundreds of recordings of his most popular works—the early piano suites, many of the lieder of 1840, the piano quintet, piano quartet, as well as the symphonies—on the market. And of course there are more online. If such numbers can be counted as indicators of popularity, then the A Minor Piano Concerto, with a remarkable 199 listings on the Arkiv.com website, would be his best-loved composition.

The *Fantasie, Carnaval, Kinderszenen,* and *Kreisleriana* are the most recorded of the early piano works, with many brilliant performances on the market. Those of *Carnaval* by Arthur Rubinstein and Arturo Benedetti Michelangeli are landmarks worth seeking out. *Kreisleriana* has, among other great versions, a legendary 1969 studio performance by Vladimir Horowitz. Yet the *Novelletten* are shamefully underrepresented, with only one complete performance by a major pianist, that by Vladimir Ashkenazy. While not quite so neglected, the *Davidsbündlertänze* still shows about half as many recordings as its better known siblings, which is why it is on the CD at the back of the book. As I have mentioned, when there are earlier and later versions of any of Schumann's compositions, you're better off finding recordings specifying the earlier one. Matthias Zimmermann's performance of the later version is quite good, though. Constraints of time unfortunately keep the sample from the E-flat Major Piano Quintet to one of its four movements, but the recording is a fine one by the Kodály Quartet, a fine

Hungarian ensemble, with pianist Jenö Jandó that's intended to whet your appetite for the full work.

Sensitivity, warmth, and intelligence mark the German baritone Andreas Schmidt's performance of *Dichterliebe*. This is another popular work of Schumann's with a crowded field of recordings. In the must-hear category is the performance by the lyric tenor Fritz Wunderlich, who died at thirty-five following an accidental fall. (You should also listen to Wunderlich's interpretation of Schubert's *Die schöne Müllerin*—and just about anything he recorded.) But it's hardly the only version of Schumann's cycle worth hearing. As noted, baritone Dietrich Fischer-Dieskau recorded *Dichterliebe* several times over his long career. In its prime his voice was sumptuous, and his intelligence and skills as a singing stage performer were always high. Another favorite version of mine is by French baritone Gérard Souzay accompanied by Dalton Baldwin. There are more fine ones, too; part of the fun of learning about music is discovering performances that speak to you.

Notes

Chapter 1

1. Friskin and Freundlich, *Music for the Piano*, 171.
2. Dubal, *Reflections from the Keyboard*, 277.
3. Ibid.
4. Quoted in Worthen, *Robert Schumann*, 64.
5. Daverio, *Robert Schumann*, 116.
6. Geck, *Robert Schumann*, 111.

Chapter 2

1. Worthen, *Robert Schumann*, 6.
2. Daverio, *Robert Schumann*, 484.
3. Worthen, *Robert Schumann*, 72–73.
4. Schonberg, *The Lives of the Great Composers*, 189.
5. Quoted in Geck, *Robert Schumann*, 141.
6. Daverio, *Robert Schumann*, 489.
7. Geck, *Robert Schumann*, 91–92.
8. Geck, *Robert Schumann*, 206.

Chapter 3

1. Daverio, Robert Schumann, 87–89
2. Rosen, *The Romantic Generation*, 226.
3. Schumann, Piano Works, Vol. 1, 118.
4. Ibid., 131.
5. Rosen, *The Romantic Generation*, 673.
6. Ibid., 678–79.
7. If this aspect of Schumann's craft interests you, read Charles Rosen's analysis on pages 100–112 of *The Romantic Generation*, but be aware that the explanation is highly technical.
8. Dubal, *Reflections from the Keyboard*, 276.
9. Quoted in Daverio, *Robert Schumann*, 164.
10. Schumann, *Complete Piano Works, Vol. 4*, 80.
11. Rosen, *Critical Entertainments*, 29.

12. See Tovey, *Chamber Music*, 161.
13. Rosen, *The Romantic Era*, 221.
14. Ibid., 31.

Chapter 5

1. Tovey, *Chamber Music*, 151–52.
2. Daverio, *Robert Schumann*, 252.

Chapter 6

1. Brian Schlotel, "The Orchestral Music," 278, in *Robert Schumann*, ed. Walker.
2. See pages 315–320 of Brian Schlotel's essay, "The Orchestral Music" in *Robert Schumann*, ed. Walker.
3. Daverio, *Robert Schumann*, 229.

Chapter 7

1. Quoted in Daverio, *Robert Schumann*, 356.

Chapter 8

1. Dietrich, Fischer-Dieskau, *Robert Schumann, Words and Music: The Vocal Compositions*, 51.
2. Sams, *The Songs of Robert Schumann*, 45–46.
3. Fischer-Dieskau, *Robert Schumann, Words and Music,* 49–50.
4. Sams, *The Songs of Robert Schumann*, 53–54.
5. Ibid., 103.
6. Fischer-Dieskau, *Robert Schumann, Words and Music*, 89.
7. Astra Desmond, *Schumann Songs*, 32.
8. Sams, "The Songs," in *Robert Schumann*, ed. Walker, 143.
9. Ibid., 135–36.
10. Komar, ed., "From Heine's Poems to Schumann's Songs," in *Dichterliebe,* 4.
11. Ibid., 15–57.
12. Sams, *The Songs of Robert Schumann*, 108–22.
13. Rosen, *The Romantic Generation*, 45–46.
14. Ibid., 219–20.
15. Fischer-Dieskau, *Robert Schumann, Words and Music*, 84.
16. Ibid., 85
17. Rosen, *Critical Entertainments*, 55–58.
18. Ibid., 208.
19. Sams, *The Songs of Robert Schumann*, 276

Selected Bibliography

Crocker, Richard L. *A History of Musical Style*. New York: Dover Publications, 1986.

Daverio, John. *Robert Schumann*. New York: Oxford University Press, 1997.

Desmond, Astra. *Schumann Songs*. Seattle: University of Washington Press, 1972.

Dubal, David. *Reflections from the Keyboard*. New York: Summit Books, 1984.

Fischer-Dieskau, Dietrich. *Robert Schumann, Words and Music: The Vocal Compositions*. Translated by Reinhard G. Pauly. Portland, OR: Amadeus Press, 1981.

Friskin, James, and Irwin Freundlich. *Music for the Piano*. New York: Dover Publications, 1975.

Geck, Martin. *Robert Schumann*. Translated by Stewart Spencer. Chicago: University of Chicago Press, 2013.

Hallmark, Rufus E. *The Genesis of Schumann's Dichterliebe*. Ann Arbor: University Microfilms International, 1978.

Howat, Roy. *The Art of French Piano Music*. New Haven: Yale University Press, 2009.

Libbey, Ted. *The NPR Listener's Encyclopedia of Classical Music*. New York: Workman Publishing, 2006.

Kennedy, Michael, ed. *The Oxford Dictionary of Music*. 2nd ed. Oxford: Oxford University Press, 1994.

Ringer, Mark. *Schubert's Theater of Song*. Milwaukee: Amadeus Press, 2009.

Rosen, Charles. *Critical Entertainments*. Cambridge: Harvard University Press, 2000.

———. *The Frontiers of Meaning*. New York: Hill and Wang, 1994.

———. *Piano Notes*. New York: The Free Press, 2002.

———. *The Romantic Generation*. Cambridge: Harvard University Press, 1995.

Sams, Eric. *The Songs of Robert Schumann*. 3rd ed. Bloomington: Indiana University Press, 1993.

Schumann, Robert. *Arabeske in C Major, Op. 18*. G. Henle Verlag, 2003.

———. *Carnaval, Op. 9*. Munich: G. Henle Verlag, 1967.

———. *Chamber Music of Robert Schumann, Edited by Clara Schumann*. New York, Dover Publications, 1981.
———. *Complete Piano Works in Six Volumes, Edited by Clara Schumann, New Commentary by Wilhelm Kempff, Vol. 1*. Wiesbaden: Breitkopf and Härtel, 1989.
———. *Complete Piano Works in Six Volumes, Edited by Clara Schumann, Vol. 2*. New York: Edwin F. Kalmus.
———. *Complete Piano Works in Six Volumes, Edited by Clara Schumann, Vol. 3*. New York: Edwin F. Kalmus.
———. *Complete Piano Works in Six Volumes, Edited by Clara Schumann, Vol. 4*. New York: Edwin F. Kalmus.
———. *Complete Symphonies in Full Score, Edited by Clara Schumann*. New York: Dover Publications, 1980.
———. *Dichterliebe: An Authoritative Score, Historical Background, Essays in Analysis, Views and Comments, ed. Arthur Komar*. New York: W. W. Norton and Co., 1971.
———. *Davidsbündlertänze, Op. 6*. G. Henle Verlag, 2006.
———. *Eighty-five Songs*. Selected by Sergius Kagen. New York: International Music.
———. *Forest Scenes, Op. 82*. G. Henle Verlag, 2001.
———. *Great Works for Piano and Orchestra*. New York: Dover Publications, 1982.
———. *Kreisleriana, Op. 16*. Munich: G. Henle Verlag, 1970.
———. *Novelettes, Op. 21, Ed. Carlo Zecchi*. Milan: Edizioni Curci, 1954.
———. *Overture, Scherzo and Finale, Op. 52, Ed. Sonja Gerlach*. Mainz: Ernst Eulenberg, 2010.
———. *Scenes from Childhood, Op. 15; Album for the Young, Op. 68*. G. Henle Verlag, 1977.
———. *Symphonic Etudes, Op. 13*. Munich: G Henle Verlag, 1971.
Sacks, Oliver. *Musicophilia*. Revised and expanded ed. New York: Vintage Books, 2008.
Tovey, Donald Francis. *Chamber Music*. Oxford: Oxford University Press, 1989.
Walker, Alan, ed. *Robert Schumann: The Man and His Music*. New York: Barnes and Noble Publishers, 1974.
Worthen, John. *Robert Schumann*. New Haven: Yale University Press, 2007.

CD Track Listing

Davidsbündlertänze, Op. 6 (35:01)

Matthias Zimmermann, piano
From Thorofon CD CTH 2152

1. *Lebhaft* (1:30)
2. *Innig* (1:40)
3. *Mit Humor* (1:21)
4. *Ungeduldig* (0:48)
5. *Einfach* (2:18)
6. *Sehr rasch* (1:44)
7. *Nicht schnell* (4:29)
8. *Frisch* (1:02)
9. *Lebhaft* (1:27)
10. *Balladenmässig, sehr rasch* (1:24)
11. *Einfach* (2:06)
12. *Mit Humor* (0:38)
13. *Wild und lustig* (2:59)
14. *Zart und singend* (2:27)
15. *Frisch* (1:54)
16. *Mit gutem Humor* (1:27)
17. *Wie aus der Ferne* (4:06)
18. *Nicht schnell* (2:08)

Kodály Quartet, Jenö Jandó, piano
From Naxos CD 8.550406

19. Piano Quartet in E-flat Major, Op. 44, second movement, *In modo d'una marcia* (8:09).

Dichterliebe, Op. 48 (31:05)

Andreas Schmidt, baritone, and Rudolf Jansen, piano
From Hänssler Classic CD 981159

20. *Im wunderschönen Monat Mai* (1:49)
21. *Aus meinen Tränen spriessen* (1:00)
22. *Die Rose, die Lilie, die Taube, die Sonne* (0:37)
23. *Wenn ich in deine Augen seh'* (1:46)
24. *Ich will meine Seele tauchen* (1:13)
25. *Im Rhein, im heiligen Strome* (2:18)
26. *Ich grolle nicht* (1:43)
27. *Und wüssten's die Blumen* (1:14)
28. *Das ist ein Flöten und Geigen* (1:32)
29. *Hör' ich das Liedchen klingen* (2:11)
30. *Ein Jüngling liebt ein Mädchen* (1:14)
31. *Am leuchtenden Sommemorgen* (2:43)
32. *Ich hab' in Traum geweinet* (2:42)
33. *Allnächtlich im Traume* (1:25)
34. *Aus alten Märchen* (2:44)
35. *Die alten, bösen Lieder* (4:54)